© 2024 by FAISAL JAMIL. All rights reserved.

Title: "The Art of Idea Generation Techniques for Entrepreneurs"

This book, along with its contents encompassing text, illustrations, images, diagrams, and other creative elements, is the exclusive property of FAISAL JAMIL and is safeguarded by copyright law.

FAISAL JAMIL asserts full ownership and retains all rights to this book. No part of this publication may be reproduced, distributed, or transmitted in any form or by any means, such as photocopying, recording, or electronic methods, without prior written consent from the copyright holder. Brief quotations in critical reviews and certain noncommercial uses permitted by copyright law are exceptions.

This copyright notice applies to all editions, formats, and translations of the book, whether in print, digital, or any other medium or technology existing now or developed in the future. Unauthorized use or infringement may result in legal action and pursuit of remedies under applicable copyright laws.

While efforts have been made to ensure accuracy and reliability, FAISAL JAMIL does not guarantee the completeness or suitability of the information. Readers are responsible for evaluating and using the content judiciously.

FAISAL JAMIL reserves the right to make changes, updates, or corrections to the book without prior notice. Inclusion of third-party materials or references does not imply endorsement or affiliation unless used under fair use principles or with proper permissions and attributions.

For permissions, inquiries, or requests regarding the book's use, please contact FAISAL JAMIL through official channels listed on their Amazon author page or provided email address.

This comprehensive copyright notice serves to protect FAISAL JAMIL'S intellectual property rights, maintain content control, and inform users about associated restrictions and permissions.

Warm regards,

FAISAL JAMIL

I Always Give's Free Copies Need Your Feedback And

Reviews Keeps In Touch!

http://www.amazon.com/author/faisal.jamil

Email: faisaljamilauthor@gmail.com

About the author

Certainly! Faisal Jamil is a multifaceted individual with a diverse set of skills and experiences. With a strong foundation in computer knowledge since childhood, he has developed a deep understanding of technology that informs his work as a content writer. Faisal also possesses digital skills, which further enhance his abilities in various digital platforms and technologies.

Beyond his professional endeavors, Faisal Jamil has also excelled in the martial arts, particularly Shotokan Karate, where he achieved the prestigious rank of first Dan black belt. This achievement speaks to his dedication, discipline, and commitment to personal growth and mastery.

In his professional life, Faisal Jamil has carved out a successful career in sales management within the Fast Moving Consumer Goods (FMCG) sector. His roles in various FMCG companies have honed his skills in strategic planning, team leadership, and business development. Faisal's ability to drive sales and achieve targets has been instrumental in his career progression, showcasing his talent for identifying opportunities and delivering results.

Faisal Jamil is also deeply interested in business investment strategies, planning, and execution. His understanding of these areas has been key to his success in the business world, allowing him to make informed decisions and implement effective strategies. His ability to navigate the complexities of investment planning and execution has set him apart as a strategic thinker and a valuable asset in any business endeavor.

Overall, Faisal Jamil is a dynamic individual who combines his passion for technology, martial arts, sales management, digital skills, and business investment strategies to achieve success in diverse fields. His journey is a testament to his versatility, resilience, and continuous pursuit of excellence.

Yours Sincerely

FAISAL JAMIL

I Always Give's Free Copies Need Your Feedback And Reviews Keeps In Touch!

https://www.amazon.com/author/faisal.jamil

Email: faisaljamilauthor@gmail.com

THE ART OF
IDEA GENERATION TECHNIQUES FOR
ENTREPRENEURS

Table of Content

Preface ---8

Introduction ---10

Chapter 1: Understanding the Importance of Ideas -------16

Chapter 2: The Entrepreneurial Mindset --------------------21

Chapter 3: Identifying Problems and Pain Points -----------27

Chapter 4: Brainstorming Techniques -------------------------34

Chapter 5: Leveraging Personal Experience and Skills ----42

Chapter 6: Market Research and Trend Analysis -----------49

Chapter 7: Networking and Collaboration -------------------57

Chapter 8: Customer Feedback and Insights ----------------65

Chapter 9: Creative Thinking Techniques --------------------73

Chapter 10: Innovation and Disruption -----------------------81

Chapter 11: Cross-Industry Innovation -----------------------88

Chapter 12: Using Technology for Idea Generation -------96

Chapter 13: Idea Validation and Feasibility ----------------103

Chapter 14: Developing a Value Proposition --------------110

Chapter 15: The Role of Business Models -------------------117

Chapter 16: Storytelling and Pitching -----------------------123

Chapter 17: Building an Idea Generation Framework ---131

Chapter 18: Overcoming Creative Blocks -------------------139

Chapter 19: Case Studies of Successful Entrepreneurs --146

Chapter 20: Continuous Improvement and Adaptation -154

Preface

In the fast-paced world of entrepreneurship, the ability to generate, refine, and implement innovative ideas is the cornerstone of success. Ideas are the seeds from which the most transformative businesses grow, and the process of nurturing these seeds into thriving enterprises is both an art and a science.

"The Art of Idea Generation Techniques for Entrepreneurs" was conceived from a deep understanding of the challenges and triumphs faced by entrepreneurs. Whether you are just starting out or are a seasoned business owner looking to inject fresh life into your ventures, this book is designed to be your companion on the journey of innovation.

Over the years, I have had the privilege of working with a diverse range of entrepreneurs, witnessing firsthand the exhilarating moments of breakthrough and the inevitable obstacles that arise. These experiences have underscored a critical truth: the most successful entrepreneurs are those who continually evolve, adapt, and remain open to new possibilities.

This book is structured to guide you through the multifaceted process of idea generation, from the initial spark of inspiration to the practical steps of implementation and continuous improvement. Each chapter delves into different aspects of this journey, offering actionable insights and proven techniques. You will find chapters dedicated to fostering an entrepreneurial mindset, leveraging personal experiences, conducting market research, and using cutting-edge technology to fuel your creativity.

In addition to theoretical knowledge, I have included real-world case studies of successful entrepreneurs who have navigated the complexities of idea generation and innovation. Their stories serve as both inspiration and practical examples, demonstrating how diverse strategies can lead to groundbreaking success.

As you embark on this journey, remember that the process of idea generation is ongoing. The landscape of business is ever-changing, and the ability to adapt and improve continuously is essential. This book aims not just to provide you with immediate tools and techniques but also to instill a mindset of perpetual innovation.

I hope "The Art of Idea Generation Techniques for Entrepreneurs" inspires you, challenges you, and ultimately helps you bring your unique ideas to life. May it be a source of guidance and encouragement as you navigate the exciting world of entrepreneurship.

Here's to your journey of endless innovation and success.

Warm regards,

FAISAL JAMIL

INTRODUCTION

In the realm of entrepreneurship, the ability to generate groundbreaking ideas is the lifeblood of innovation and success. Every iconic business, from the smallest startup to the largest multinational corporation, began with a single idea—a spark of inspiration that set the foundation for what was to come. The journey from that initial spark to a thriving enterprise is often a complex and challenging process, but it is also one of the most rewarding endeavors an individual can undertake.

"The Art of Idea Generation Techniques for Entrepreneurs" is crafted to be your comprehensive guide through this journey. This book is not just about finding that first great idea; it is about creating a continuous flow of innovative concepts that can propel your business forward in an ever-evolving market landscape.

The Essence of Idea Generation

At its core, idea generation is about creativity and problem-solving. It involves looking at the world through a lens of curiosity, identifying gaps and opportunities, and envisioning solutions that can address unmet needs. This process requires a unique blend of skills, including critical thinking, adaptability, and the ability to take calculated risks.

Why This Book?

In my years of experience working with entrepreneurs across various industries, I have seen the transformative power of a well-nurtured idea. However, I have also observed the struggles that many face in consistently coming up with new and viable concepts. This book is born out of a desire to demystify the process of idea generation and provide entrepreneurs with practical tools and strategies that can be applied in real-world scenarios.

What You Will Learn

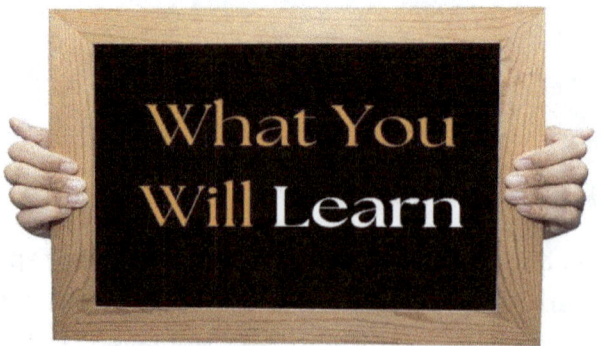

This book is structured into twenty insightful chapters, each focusing on different aspects of idea generation and entrepreneurial success:

1: Understanding the Importance of Ideas: Exploring the foundational role of ideas in entrepreneurship.

2: The Entrepreneurial Mindset: Cultivating the traits needed for innovative thinking.

3: Identifying Problems and Pain Points: Techniques for uncovering market needs.

4: Brainstorming Techniques: Diverse methods for generating a wealth of ideas.

5: Leveraging Personal Experience and Skills: Using your background to inspire unique concepts.

6: Market Research and Trend Analysis: Understanding the market to inform your ideas.

7: Networking and Collaboration: The power of connecting with others.

8: Customer Feedback and Insights: Gathering and interpreting feedback to refine ideas.

9: Creative Thinking Techniques: Tools to enhance your creative process.

10: Innovation and Disruption: Generating ideas that challenge the status quo.

11: Cross-Industry Innovation: Adapting successful concepts from other fields.

12: Using Technology for Idea Generation: Leveraging tools and platforms to fuel creativity.

13: Idea Validation and Feasibility: Assessing and validating your ideas.

14: Developing a Value Proposition: Crafting a compelling value proposition.

15: The Role of Business Models: Choosing the right business model for your idea.

16: Storytelling and Pitching: Communicating your idea effectively.

17: Building an Idea Generation Framework: Systematic approaches to consistent innovation.

18: Overcoming Creative Blocks: Strategies to overcome obstacles in your creative process.

19: Case Studies of Successful Entrepreneurs: Learning from the successes of others.

20: Continuous Improvement and Adaptation: The importance of evolving your ideas and business.

Embarking on Your Journey

As you read through the chapters, you will discover a blend of theoretical insights and practical advice designed to ignite your creativity and enhance your entrepreneurial capabilities. Whether you are at the beginning of your entrepreneurial journey or seeking to rejuvenate an existing business, this book aims to equip you with the knowledge and inspiration needed to thrive.

Innovation is a journey, not a destination. By embracing the art of idea generation, you are committing to a path of continuous growth and endless possibilities. Let this book be your guide as you navigate the exciting world of entrepreneurship, turning your ideas into impactful and successful ventures.

Welcome to "The Art of Idea Generation Techniques for Entrepreneurs." Let's embark on this journey of innovation together.

Warm regards,

FAISAL JAMIL

Chapter 1
Understanding the
Importance of Ideas

The Foundation of Success

In the world of entrepreneurship, ideas are the bedrock upon which successful businesses are built. Every innovative company, from tech giants like Apple and Google to small local startups, began with a single idea. This idea serves as the seed that, with proper nurturing and development, can grow into a profitable and impactful venture. Understanding the importance of ideas is crucial for any aspiring entrepreneur because it is this initial spark that drives the entire entrepreneurial journey.

The Role of Ideas in Entrepreneurship

1: Inspiration and Motivation: A great idea provides the inspiration and motivation needed to embark on the challenging path of entrepreneurship. It ignites a passion within the entrepreneur, fueling their drive to turn the idea into reality.

2: Direction and Focus: Ideas give direction and focus to entrepreneurial efforts. They help define the mission and vision of the business, guiding strategic decisions and actions. Without a clear idea, efforts can become scattered and unproductive.

3: Innovation and Differentiation: In a competitive market, innovative ideas are key to differentiation. They allow businesses to stand out by offering unique solutions to problems, thereby attracting customers and creating a competitive edge.

The Seed of a Profitable Venture

Just as a seed requires the right conditions to grow into a healthy plant, an idea needs careful nurturing and development to become a successful business. This involves several steps:

1: Refinement: Initial ideas are often raw and need refinement. This process involves critically evaluating the idea, seeking feedback, and iterating on it to improve its viability and potential impact.

2: Validation: Validating an idea involves testing it in the real world to ensure there is a market need and demand for it. This can be done through market research, surveys, and pilot testing.

3: Implementation: Turning an idea into a reality requires a detailed plan and execution. This includes developing a business model, securing funding, building a team, and launching the product or service.

Vision: The Driving Force Behind Ideas

A strong vision is essential for transforming an idea into a successful business. Vision is the ability to see beyond the present and imagine what the future could look like. It involves:

1: Seeing Opportunities: Visionary entrepreneurs have a knack for spotting opportunities where others see challenges. They can identify gaps in the market, emerging trends, and unmet needs that their ideas can address.

2: Strategic Planning: A clear vision helps in strategic planning. It allows entrepreneurs to set long-term goals, make informed decisions, and stay focused on their mission even when faced with obstacles.

3: Inspiring Others: Vision is also crucial for inspiring and rallying others around the idea. Whether it's attracting investors, building a team, or convincing customers, a compelling vision can galvanize support and enthusiasm.

Spotting Opportunities in the Market

To generate impactful ideas, entrepreneurs need to develop the ability to spot opportunities in the market. This involves:

1: Market Research: Conducting thorough market research to understand current trends, consumer behavior, and gaps in the market. Tools such as surveys, focus groups, and data analysis are invaluable in this process.

2: Observing Pain Points: Identifying common pain points and challenges faced by consumers can reveal opportunities for innovative solutions. Engaging with potential customers and listening to their needs is critical.

3: Staying Informed: Keeping abreast of industry developments, technological advancements, and societal changes can help entrepreneurs stay ahead of the curve and identify new opportunities early.

Case Study: Airbnb

To illustrate the importance of ideas, vision, and opportunity spotting, consider the case of Airbnb. The idea for Airbnb was born when its founders noticed a significant pain point: people struggling to find affordable and unique accommodation options, especially during peak travel times. Their vision was to create a platform that allowed people to rent out their spare rooms or homes to travelers, providing a more personal and cost-effective alternative to traditional hotels.

By conducting market research and observing trends in the sharing economy, the founders refined their idea and launched Airbnb. Their ability to spot this opportunity, coupled with a strong vision and strategic planning, transformed Airbnb into a global hospitality giant, revolutionizing the travel industry.

Conclusion

Understanding the importance of ideas in entrepreneurship is the first step towards building a successful business. Ideas are the seeds that, when combined with a strong vision and the ability to spot opportunities, can grow into impactful and profitable ventures. Aspiring entrepreneurs must cultivate their creativity, stay curious, and continuously seek out new ideas and opportunities to turn their entrepreneurial dreams into reality.

Chapter 2
The Entrepreneurial Mindset

The Essence of an Entrepreneurial Mindset

Successful entrepreneurs share a distinctive mindset that sets them apart. This mindset is characterized by several key traits that enable them to generate innovative ideas, overcome obstacles, and thrive in the competitive world of business. Developing an entrepreneurial mindset is crucial for anyone aspiring to become a successful entrepreneur.

Characteristics of an Entrepreneurial Mindset

1: Curiosity

Definition: Curiosity is the desire to learn, explore, and understand new things. It drives entrepreneurs to ask questions, seek new knowledge, and challenge the status quo.

Importance: Curiosity fuels innovation by encouraging entrepreneurs to look beyond the obvious and explore new possibilities. It leads to the discovery of new opportunities and the development of creative solutions to problems.

Cultivation: Entrepreneurs can cultivate curiosity by reading widely, engaging in diverse experiences, and maintaining an open mind. Networking with people from different backgrounds and industries can also stimulate curiosity and inspire new ideas.

2: Resilience

Definition: Resilience is the ability to bounce back from setbacks and persist in the face of challenges. It is about maintaining a positive attitude and staying focused on goals despite difficulties.

Importance: Entrepreneurship is fraught with obstacles and failures. Resilience is crucial for overcoming these challenges and continuing to move forward. It helps entrepreneurs learn from failures, adapt to changing circumstances, and remain committed to their vision.

Cultivation: Building resilience involves developing a growth mindset, where failures are viewed as learning opportunities rather than defeats. Entrepreneurs can also strengthen resilience by setting realistic goals, seeking support from mentors and peers, and practicing stress management techniques.

3: Willingness to Take Risks

Definition: Taking risks involves stepping out of one's comfort zone and venturing into the unknown. It requires a willingness to face uncertainty and potential failure.

Importance: Risk-taking is inherent to entrepreneurship. It is through taking calculated risks that entrepreneurs can seize new opportunities, innovate, and achieve significant growth. Risk-averse behavior can limit potential and stifle creativity.

Cultivation: Entrepreneurs can develop a healthy risk appetite by conducting thorough research and analysis before making decisions. They should weigh potential risks against potential rewards and develop contingency plans. Building confidence through small, incremental risks can also prepare entrepreneurs for larger, more significant risks.

Cultivating an Entrepreneurial Mindset

1: Continuous Learning

Importance: The business landscape is constantly evolving, and staying informed is essential for generating new ideas and staying competitive. Continuous learning helps entrepreneurs adapt to changes, acquire new skills, and remain innovative.

Methods: Entrepreneurs can engage in continuous learning through formal education, online courses, workshops, and seminars. Reading books, articles, and industry reports, as well as listening to podcasts and watching webinars, are also effective ways to stay updated.

2: Adaptability

Definition: Adaptability is the ability to adjust to new conditions and modify plans in response to changing circumstances. It involves being flexible and open to change.

Importance: The entrepreneurial journey is unpredictable, and adaptability is crucial for navigating uncertainties. Entrepreneurs who can quickly pivot and adjust their strategies are better positioned to capitalize on new opportunities and mitigate risks.

Cultivation: Entrepreneurs can develop adaptability by practicing mindfulness and staying present in the moment. This helps in being more aware of changes and responding proactively. Embracing a culture of experimentation and being willing to iterate on ideas and approaches also fosters adaptability.

3: Networking and Collaboration

Importance: Building a strong network and collaborating with others can provide valuable insights, support, and resources. It exposes entrepreneurs to diverse perspectives and ideas, fostering innovation and growth.

Methods: Entrepreneurs can expand their network by attending industry events, joining professional organizations, and participating in online communities. Building meaningful relationships and seeking out mentors can also provide guidance and inspiration.

4: Embracing Failure as a Learning Opportunity

Importance: Failure is an inevitable part of the entrepreneurial journey. Viewing failure as a learning opportunity rather than a setback allows entrepreneurs to gain valuable insights and improve their strategies.

Methods: Entrepreneurs should conduct post-mortems after failures to analyze what went wrong and identify lessons learned. Maintaining a positive attitude and resilience in the face of failure is crucial for continuous improvement and growth.

Case Study: Elon Musk

Elon Musk, the founder of companies like Tesla, SpaceX, and Neuralink, exemplifies the entrepreneurial mindset. His insatiable curiosity drives him to explore diverse fields, from electric vehicles to space exploration. Musk's resilience is evident in his ability to overcome numerous setbacks, including the early failures of SpaceX rockets. His willingness to take risks is unparalleled, investing his personal fortune into ventures others deemed too risky.

Musk continuously learns and adapts, staying ahead of industry trends and technological advancements. He leverages his extensive network and collaborates with experts across various fields. Importantly, Musk embraces failure, using it as a stepping stone for future success. His mindset has enabled him to generate groundbreaking ideas and revolutionize multiple industries.

Conclusion

Developing an entrepreneurial mindset is essential for generating innovative ideas and achieving success in the world of entrepreneurship. Curiosity, resilience, and a willingness to take risks are key characteristics that drive entrepreneurs to explore new possibilities, overcome challenges, and seize opportunities. Cultivating this mindset through continuous learning, adaptability, networking, and embracing failure can empower aspiring entrepreneurs to navigate the dynamic business landscape and turn their ideas into reality.

Chapter 3
Identifying Problems and Pain Points

The Origin of Great Ideas

In the entrepreneurial world, great ideas often emerge from identifying and solving problems. Problems and pain points present opportunities for innovation and value creation. By addressing these issues, entrepreneurs can develop products and services that meet real needs, attract customers, and build successful businesses.

Understanding Problems and Pain Points

1: Problems

Definition: Problems are obstacles or challenges that individuals or businesses face. These can range from minor inconveniences to significant issues that hinder performance or satisfaction.

Relevance: Identifying problems provides a foundation for developing solutions that improve lives or business processes.

2: Pain Points

Definition: Pain points are specific issues that cause frustration, inconvenience, or inefficiency for people or organizations. These are often more immediate and tangible than broader problems.

Relevance: Addressing pain points directly can lead to higher customer satisfaction and loyalty, as it resolves pressing issues that impact daily life or operations.

Techniques for Identifying Problems and Pain Points

1: Observation

Importance: Observing people in their natural environments provides insights into their behaviors, challenges, and needs that might not be evident through other methods.

Methods: Entrepreneurs can conduct field research by visiting places where potential customers spend time. For example, observing shoppers in a retail store can reveal inefficiencies in the shopping experience. Ethnographic research, where entrepreneurs immerse themselves in the target audience's environment, is also valuable.

2: Surveys

Importance: Surveys allow entrepreneurs to gather quantitative data on a large scale, helping identify common problems and pain points experienced by a target audience.

Methods: Designing effective surveys involves creating clear, concise questions that elicit meaningful responses. Using online survey tools, entrepreneurs can distribute surveys to a broad audience and analyze the results to identify patterns and trends.

3: Interviews

Importance: Interviews provide in-depth, qualitative insights into individuals' experiences, thoughts, and emotions regarding specific issues.

Methods: Conducting one-on-one interviews with potential customers or industry experts can uncover nuanced pain points and problems. Entrepreneurs should prepare open-ended questions and actively listen to responses, probing deeper to understand underlying issues.

4: Focus Groups

Importance: Focus groups facilitate discussions among a group of people, providing diverse perspectives on specific topics or problems.

Methods: Organizing focus group sessions involves gathering a representative sample of the target audience and moderating discussions around key themes. This technique helps identify common pain points and potential solutions through collective brainstorming and dialogue.

5: Customer Feedback

Importance: Existing customers are a valuable source of information about pain points related to current products or services.

Methods: Entrepreneurs can gather feedback through reviews, customer service interactions, and feedback forms. Analyzing this feedback helps identify recurring issues and areas for improvement.

6: Competitive Analysis

Importance: Studying competitors can reveal gaps in the market and areas where existing solutions fall short, presenting opportunities for innovation.

Methods: Entrepreneurs can conduct competitive analysis by reviewing competitors' products, services, customer reviews, and marketing strategies. Identifying weaknesses or unmet needs in competitors' offerings can inspire new ideas.

Case Study: Slack

Slack, a leading communication platform, originated from identifying a common pain point: inefficient team communication. The founders observed the fragmented and cumbersome nature of email and other communication tools used in workplaces. By conducting surveys and interviews with potential users, they uncovered specific pain points related to information overload, lack of real-time collaboration, and difficulty in tracking conversations.

Through these insights, Slack developed a platform that addressed these pain points by providing a centralized, real-time messaging solution with features like channels, file sharing, and integrations with other tools. Slack's success underscores the importance of identifying and addressing pain points to create impactful solutions.

Applying Techniques to Identify Problems and Pain Points

1: Observation in Action

Entrepreneurs looking to develop a new retail technology might spend time observing shoppers in stores, noting frustrations like long checkout lines, difficulty finding products, or lack of personalized assistance. These observations can highlight pain points that a new technology could address, such as self-checkout kiosks or mobile apps for personalized shopping experiences.

2: Surveys for Market Insights

An entrepreneur interested in the fitness industry might distribute surveys to gym-goers to understand their challenges. Questions could explore issues like scheduling difficulties, lack of motivation, or inadequate access to personalized training. Survey results might reveal that many gym-goers struggle with finding time for workouts, leading to the development of a flexible, on-demand fitness app.

3: Interviews for Deep Understanding

In the healthcare sector, an entrepreneur might conduct interviews with patients and healthcare providers to uncover pain points related to medical appointments. Through interviews, they might discover issues such as long wait times, difficulty in booking appointments, or lack of communication between providers and patients. These insights could inform the creation of a more efficient healthcare scheduling and communication platform.

4: Focus Groups for Collaborative Insights

For a new educational tool, an entrepreneur might organize focus groups with teachers and students to discuss challenges in the learning process. Discussions might reveal pain points like lack of engagement, difficulty in accessing resources, or inadequate feedback mechanisms. These insights could inspire the development of an interactive and resource-rich educational platform.

5: Customer Feedback for Continuous Improvement

An entrepreneur with an existing e-commerce business might analyze customer feedback to identify pain points related to the shopping experience. Feedback might highlight issues like slow website performance, limited payment options, or poor customer service. Addressing these pain points could lead to improvements that enhance customer satisfaction and loyalty.

6: Competitive Analysis for Market Gaps

In the transportation industry, an entrepreneur might analyze ride-sharing competitors to identify unmet needs.

They might find that existing services lack options for larger groups or accessible vehicles for people with disabilities. These insights could drive the development of a more inclusive and versatile ride-sharing service.

Conclusion

Identifying problems and pain points is a crucial step in the entrepreneurial journey. By employing techniques such as observation, surveys, interviews, focus groups, customer feedback, and competitive analysis, entrepreneurs can uncover unmet needs and develop innovative solutions that address these challenges. This approach not only leads to the creation of valuable products and services but also ensures that the solutions resonate with the target audience, ultimately driving business success.

Chapter 4
Brainstorming Techniques

The Power of Brainstorming

Brainstorming is a time-tested method for generating ideas and fostering creativity. It allows individuals or groups to explore a wide range of possibilities, break through mental barriers, and discover innovative solutions. By leveraging various brainstorming techniques, entrepreneurs can unlock their creative potential and develop impactful ideas for their ventures.

The Brainstorming Process

Effective brainstorming involves creating an open and encouraging environment where participants feel free to express their thoughts without judgment. The process typically follows these steps:

1: Preparation: Define the problem or challenge clearly. Gather the necessary materials, such as whiteboards, sticky notes, or digital tools, and ensure a comfortable space for participants.

2: Divergence: Encourage participants to generate as many ideas as possible without evaluating them. This phase focuses on quantity, not quality.

3: Convergence: After the initial idea generation, evaluate and refine the ideas, identifying the most promising ones for further development.

Popular Brainstorming Techniques

1. Mind Mapping

Definition: Mind mapping is a visual brainstorming technique that organizes ideas around a central concept. It uses branches to represent related ideas, creating a hierarchical structure.

How to Use:

Start with a central idea or problem in the middle of a blank page or digital tool.

Draw branches from the central idea, representing different aspects or components.

Add sub-branches to each main branch, detailing related ideas or solutions.

Use colors, images, and keywords to enhance the map's clarity and stimulate creativity.

Benefits: Mind mapping helps visualize connections between ideas, making it easier to see relationships and develop comprehensive solutions. It also engages both the logical and creative sides of the brain.

Example: An entrepreneur brainstorming a new fitness app might start with "Fitness App" as the central idea. Main branches could include "Features," "Target Audience," "Marketing Strategies," and "Technology." Sub-branches under "Features" might include "Workout Plans," "Nutrition Tracking," and "Community Support."

2. Free Writing

Definition: Free writing is a technique where participants write continuously for a set period without worrying about grammar, spelling, or coherence. The goal is to capture raw ideas and thoughts.

How to Use:

Set a timer (e.g., 10-15 minutes).

Start writing about the topic or problem without stopping.

Allow thoughts to flow freely, capturing everything that comes to mind.

Review the written content afterward to identify useful ideas or patterns.

Benefits: Free writing bypasses the inner critic, allowing for unfiltered expression of ideas. It can reveal subconscious thoughts and spark new insights.

Example: An entrepreneur might set a timer for 15 minutes and write nonstop about potential features for a new productivity tool. Reviewing the text afterward might reveal unexpected and innovative feature ideas.

3. SCAMPER Method

Definition: The SCAMPER method is a structured brainstorming technique that prompts creative thinking by encouraging participants to apply seven different actions to an existing idea or problem. SCAMPER stands for Substitute, Combine, Adapt, Modify, Put to another use, Eliminate, and Reverse.

How to Use:

Substitute: What can be replaced or used instead? (e.g., materials, processes, people)

Combine: What can be combined to create something new? (e.g., ideas, products, services)

Adapt: What can be adapted or adjusted to improve? (e.g., methods, designs)

Modify: What can be changed or altered? (e.g., size, shape, features)

Put to another use: How can the idea be used differently? (e.g., repurpose, new applications)

Eliminate: What can be removed or simplified? (e.g., steps, components)

Reverse: What can be reversed or done in the opposite way? (e.g., processes, roles)

Benefits: SCAMPER provides a systematic approach to brainstorming, ensuring a thorough exploration of possibilities. It encourages thinking beyond conventional solutions.

Example: An entrepreneur developing a new type of reusable water bottle might use SCAMPER:

Substitute: Replace plastic with a more sustainable material.

Combine: Combine a water bottle with a built-in filter.

Adapt: Adapt the bottle's design for easier cleaning.

Modify: Modify the shape for better grip.

Put to another use: Use the bottle as a storage container for other liquids.

Eliminate: Remove unnecessary components to simplify the design.

Reverse: Reverse the opening mechanism for better usability.

4. Brainwriting

Definition: Brainwriting is a silent brainstorming technique where participants write down their ideas instead of speaking them aloud. It allows for equal participation and prevents dominant voices from overshadowing others.

How to Use:

Provide each participant with a sheet of paper or digital form.

Set a timer for a few minutes.

Have participants write down their ideas individually.

After the time is up, participants pass their sheets to the next person, who reads and adds to the ideas.

Repeat the process for several rounds, then review and discuss the compiled ideas.

Benefits: Brainwriting encourages participation from all group members, reduces the pressure of immediate verbal responses, and generates a diverse set of ideas.

Example: In a session to brainstorm marketing strategies for a new product, each team member writes down their ideas, then passes their sheets around for others to build upon. This process continues for several rounds, resulting in a rich collection of strategies to evaluate.

5. Role Storming

Definition: Role storming involves participants assuming different personas or roles while brainstorming. By stepping into someone else's shoes, participants can explore new perspectives and generate unique ideas.

How to Use:

Define the problem or challenge.

Assign different roles or personas to participants (e.g., a customer, competitor, industry expert, child).

Have participants brainstorm ideas from the perspective of their assigned roles.

Share and discuss the ideas generated from each perspective.

Benefits: Role storming fosters empathy and helps uncover insights that might be missed when thinking from a single perspective. It encourages creative thinking by breaking habitual thought patterns.

Example: An entrepreneur developing a new educational toy might have participants assume roles such as a child, parent, teacher, and toy manufacturer. Each role provides different insights into the features, design, and marketing of the toy.

Case Study: IDEO

IDEO, a global design and innovation firm, is renowned for its creative brainstorming techniques. When tasked with redesigning the shopping cart, IDEO employed various brainstorming methods to generate innovative ideas. They used mind mapping to explore different aspects of the shopping experience, role storming to understand perspectives of shoppers and store employees, and the SCAMPER method to rethink existing cart designs.

By leveraging these techniques, IDEO's team generated numerous ideas, ultimately creating a revolutionary shopping cart design that improved safety, convenience, and efficiency. This case study highlights the power of diverse brainstorming techniques in generating breakthrough solutions.

Conclusion

Brainstorming is a powerful tool for generating innovative ideas and solving problems. Techniques like mind mapping, free writing, the SCAMPER method, brainwriting, and role storming provide structured approaches to creative thinking, enabling entrepreneurs to explore a wide range of possibilities. By mastering these techniques, entrepreneurs can unlock their creative potential, develop impactful solutions, and drive their ventures toward success.

Chapter 5
Leveraging Personal Experience and Skills

The Value of Personal Experience and Skills

Personal experiences and skills are invaluable assets in the entrepreneurial journey. They provide unique insights, perspectives, and competencies that can inspire innovative business ideas. By tapping into their background, knowledge, and hobbies, entrepreneurs can create ventures that are not only unique but also aligned with their passions and strengths.

Identifying Relevant Experiences and Skills

1: Reflecting on Past Experiences

Importance: Reflecting on past experiences helps entrepreneurs identify situations where they encountered problems, overcame challenges, or achieved successes. These reflections can reveal patterns and insights that inspire business ideas.

Methods: Entrepreneurs can use journaling or mind mapping to document significant experiences in their personal and professional lives. Analyzing these experiences can uncover unmet needs or opportunities for innovation.

2: Assessing Skills and Expertise

Importance: Understanding one's skills and expertise allows entrepreneurs to leverage their strengths in developing business ideas. Skills can range from technical abilities to soft skills like communication and leadership.

Methods: Entrepreneurs can create a skills inventory, listing all their competencies and areas of expertise. They should consider both hard skills (e.g., programming, graphic design) and soft skills (e.g., problem-solving, teamwork).

3: Exploring Hobbies and Interests

Importance: Hobbies and interests often reflect personal passions and can be a source of creative inspiration. Leveraging these interests can lead to business ideas that are both fulfilling and engaging.

Methods: Entrepreneurs can list their hobbies and interests and brainstorm how these activities might translate into business opportunities. For example, a passion for photography could inspire a business in photography services, equipment, or education.

Leveraging Personal Background

1: Professional Experience

Importance: Professional experience provides industry-specific knowledge and insights that can be invaluable in identifying market gaps and opportunities.

Methods: Entrepreneurs can analyze their career history to identify skills, knowledge, and networks they can leverage. They should consider how their professional background can be applied to new contexts or markets.

Example: An entrepreneur with a background in healthcare might identify inefficiencies in patient management systems. Their expertise could inspire the development of a streamlined healthcare software solution.

2: Life Experiences

Importance: Personal life experiences, such as overcoming adversity or managing personal projects, can offer unique perspectives and resilience that are beneficial in entrepreneurship.

Methods: Entrepreneurs can reflect on significant life events and consider how these experiences have shaped their problem-solving abilities and worldview. They should explore how these insights can be translated into business ideas.

Example: An entrepreneur who has navigated the challenges of raising a child with special needs might develop products or services that support families in similar situations.

Leveraging Skills and Knowledge

1: Technical Skills

Importance: Technical skills enable entrepreneurs to develop innovative products or services that require specialized knowledge.

Methods: Entrepreneurs can brainstorm business ideas that utilize their technical skills. They should consider how their expertise can solve problems or meet needs in new and creative ways.

Example: A software developer might create a new app that addresses a common issue they've encountered, such as project management or personal finance tracking.

2: Soft Skills

Importance: Soft skills like communication, leadership, and empathy are crucial for building and managing a successful business.

Methods: Entrepreneurs can identify how their soft skills can enhance customer relationships, team dynamics, or marketing strategies. They should think about how these skills can differentiate their business in the market.

Example: An entrepreneur with strong leadership skills might focus on creating a company culture that attracts top talent and fosters innovation.

Leveraging Hobbies and Interests

1: Turning Passions into Profits

Importance: Turning hobbies and passions into a business allows entrepreneurs to work on something they love, increasing motivation and satisfaction.

Methods: Entrepreneurs can explore how their hobbies can meet market needs or solve problems. They should research the market to identify potential opportunities and validate their ideas.

Example: A gardening enthusiast might start a business selling unique plant varieties, gardening tools, or offering landscaping services.

2: Innovating Within Familiar Arenas

Importance: Hobbies often provide deep knowledge and a fresh perspective on niche markets, which can lead to innovative business ideas.

Methods: Entrepreneurs can analyze trends and challenges within their hobbies and think about how they can offer unique solutions or improvements.

Example: A home brewer might create a business around custom brewing kits or unique beer recipes, leveraging their hobby to tap into the growing craft beer market.

Combining Experiences and Skills

1: Cross-Industry Innovation

Importance: Combining knowledge and skills from different industries can lead to groundbreaking ideas and solutions that bridge gaps between fields.

Methods: Entrepreneurs can identify synergies between their varied experiences and skills. They should brainstorm ways to apply principles or techniques from one industry to another.

Example: An entrepreneur with experience in both finance and education might develop a financial literacy program tailored for schools, combining their expertise to address a critical need.

2: Creating Unique Value Propositions

Importance: A unique combination of experiences and skills can differentiate a business in the market, offering a value proposition that competitors cannot easily replicate.

Methods: Entrepreneurs can articulate how their unique background and skills set their business apart. They should focus on how this unique combination benefits customers and solves their problems in novel ways.

Example: An entrepreneur with a background in psychology and marketing might create a marketing consultancy that uses psychological insights to develop more effective advertising campaigns.

Case Study: Spanx by Sara Blakely

Sara Blakely, the founder of Spanx, leveraged her personal experiences and skills to create a revolutionary product. Blakely's experience selling fax machines gave her insights into sales and marketing, while her personal frustration with traditional undergarments inspired her to create a more comfortable and flattering alternative. She combined her knowledge of sales with her understanding of consumer needs to develop Spanx, a product that addressed a common pain point for women. Blakely's ability to leverage her experiences and skills was key to her success, transforming Spanx into a billion-dollar company.

Conclusion

Leveraging personal experiences and skills is a powerful strategy for generating unique and impactful business ideas. By reflecting on their background, assessing their skills, and exploring their hobbies and interests, entrepreneurs can identify opportunities that align with their passions and strengths. This approach not only fosters innovation but also ensures that the entrepreneurial journey is both fulfilling and rewarding. Aspiring entrepreneurs should continuously seek to integrate their unique experiences and skills into their idea generation process, creating ventures that stand out in the market and resonate with their target audience.

Chapter 6
Market Research and Trend Analysis

The Importance of Market Research and Trend Analysis

In the entrepreneurial world, understanding market trends and consumer behavior is crucial for generating relevant and innovative business ideas. Market research and trend analysis help entrepreneurs identify opportunities, anticipate changes, and make informed decisions. This chapter delves into methods for conducting market research and analyzing trends, leveraging online tools and data analysis to generate actionable insights.

Conducting Market Research

1: Defining Objectives and Scope

Importance: Clear objectives and a well-defined scope ensure that the market research process is focused and relevant. This step helps in determining what information is needed and how to gather it effectively.

Methods: Entrepreneurs should outline specific goals, such as understanding consumer needs, identifying market gaps, or analyzing competitor strategies. They should also define the scope, including the target market, geographic area, and time frame.

2: Primary Research

Importance: Primary research involves collecting original data directly from sources, providing firsthand insights into consumer behavior, preferences, and attitudes.

Methods: Techniques for primary research include:

Surveys: Online or offline questionnaires that gather quantitative data from a large sample of respondents.

Interviews: In-depth, qualitative discussions with individuals to explore their experiences and opinions.

Focus Groups: Group discussions that provide diverse perspectives on a specific topic or product.

Observations: Watching and recording behaviors in natural settings to understand how consumers interact with products or services.

3: Secondary Research

Importance: Secondary research involves analyzing existing data and information, offering a cost-effective way to gather market insights.

Methods: Sources for secondary research include:

Industry Reports: Comprehensive studies conducted by research firms that provide detailed analysis of market conditions, trends, and forecasts.

Academic Journals: Peer-reviewed publications that offer theoretical and empirical research on various market-related topics.

Government Publications: Statistical data and reports published by government agencies, such as census data, economic indicators, and trade statistics.

Online Databases: Repositories of market data and reports, such as Statista, IBISWorld, and MarketResearch.com.

4: Competitive Analysis

Importance: Analyzing competitors helps entrepreneurs understand the competitive landscape, identify strengths and weaknesses, and uncover opportunities for differentiation.

Methods: Techniques for competitive analysis include:

SWOT Analysis: Evaluating competitors' strengths, weaknesses, opportunities, and threats.

Benchmarking: Comparing competitors' performance metrics to industry standards.

Mystery Shopping: Posing as a customer to assess competitors' products, services, and customer experience.

Review Analysis: Analyzing customer reviews and feedback on competitors' offerings to identify common praises and complaints.

Analyzing Market Trends

1: Trend Identification

Importance: Identifying emerging trends helps entrepreneurs stay ahead of the curve and capitalize on new opportunities.

Methods: Techniques for identifying trends include:

Social Media Monitoring: Analyzing conversations and hashtags on platforms like Twitter, Instagram, and LinkedIn to spot emerging topics and consumer sentiments.

Google Trends: Using Google's tool to track the popularity of search terms over time, providing insights into what people are interested in.

News and Industry Publications: Keeping up with industry-specific news, blogs, and magazines to stay informed about recent developments and trends.

Trade Shows and Conferences: Attending industry events to network with experts, observe innovations, and gather insights on the latest trends.

2: Data Analysis

Importance: Analyzing data helps entrepreneurs make sense of large volumes of information and identify patterns that can inform business decisions.

Methods: Techniques for data analysis include:

Descriptive Analysis: Summarizing data to understand its main characteristics, using measures such as mean, median, and mode.

Trend Analysis: Examining data over time to identify patterns, peaks, and troughs that indicate trends.

Predictive Analysis: Using statistical models and algorithms to forecast future trends based on historical data.

Sentiment Analysis: Analyzing text data from social media, reviews, and surveys to gauge consumer sentiment and emotions.

3: Market Segmentation

Importance: Segmenting the market allows entrepreneurs to target specific groups of consumers with tailored products and marketing strategies.

Methods: Techniques for market segmentation include:

Demographic Segmentation: Dividing the market based on demographic factors such as age, gender, income, education, and occupation.

Geographic Segmentation: Segmenting the market based on geographic factors such as region, city, climate, and population density.

Psychographic Segmentation: Segmenting the market based on lifestyle, values, attitudes, and personality traits.

Behavioral Segmentation: Dividing the market based on consumer behaviors, such as purchase frequency, brand loyalty, and usage patterns.

Leveraging Online Tools for Market Research and Trend Analysis

1: Survey Tools

Examples: SurveyMonkey, Google Forms, Typeform

Benefits: These tools enable entrepreneurs to create and distribute surveys easily, collect responses, and analyze data in real-time.

2: Analytics Tools

Examples: Google Analytics, HubSpot, Kissmetrics

Benefits: These tools provide insights into website traffic, user behavior, and marketing effectiveness, helping entrepreneurs understand how consumers interact with their online presence.

3: Social Media Monitoring Tools

Examples: Hootsuite, Sprout Social, Brandwatch

Benefits: These tools help entrepreneurs track social media conversations, measure engagement, and analyze sentiment, providing a real-time pulse on consumer trends and opinions.

4: Market Research Platforms

Examples: Statista, IBISWorld, MarketResearch.com

Benefits: These platforms offer access to comprehensive market reports, industry statistics, and trend analyses, providing a wealth of information for informed decision-making.

Case Study: Airbnb

Airbnb's success story illustrates the importance of market research and trend analysis. Founders Brian Chesky and Joe Gebbia initially identified a growing trend in the sharing economy and a demand for affordable, unique lodging options. They conducted extensive market research, including surveys and interviews with potential users, to understand consumer preferences and pain points in the travel accommodation industry.

By leveraging online tools and data analysis, they identified key trends such as the rise of peer-to-peer platforms, the desire for authentic travel experiences, and the increasing use of digital technologies in travel planning. This informed their business model and product development, leading to the creation of a platform that revolutionized the hospitality industry.

Conclusion

Market research and trend analysis are critical components of the entrepreneurial process. By understanding market trends and consumer behavior, entrepreneurs can generate relevant and innovative business ideas that meet real needs and capitalize on emerging opportunities. Conducting thorough research using primary and secondary methods, analyzing data, and leveraging online tools are essential steps in this process. Armed with these insights, entrepreneurs can make informed decisions, reduce risks, and increase the likelihood of success in their ventures.

Chapter 7
Networking and Collaboration

The Power of Networking and Collaboration

Networking and collaboration are vital components of entrepreneurial success. By connecting with other entrepreneurs, industry experts, and potential partners, entrepreneurs can gain fresh perspectives, access new resources, and spark innovative ideas. This chapter emphasizes the importance of building a strong network and offers practical tips on how to effectively collaborate with others.

The Importance of Networking

1: Access to Diverse Perspectives

Importance: Engaging with a diverse network provides exposure to different viewpoints, ideas, and experiences, which can inspire creativity and innovation.

Methods: Attend industry events, join professional associations, and participate in online forums to interact with a variety of individuals.

2: Opportunities for Collaboration

Importance: Collaboration can lead to new business opportunities, partnerships, and ventures that might not be possible when working alone.

Methods: Identify potential collaborators through networking events, social media, and industry-specific platforms. Approach them with clear value propositions and mutual benefits.

3: Knowledge Sharing and Learning

Importance: Networking allows entrepreneurs to learn from others' successes and failures, gaining valuable insights and avoiding common pitfalls.

Methods: Engage in discussions, attend workshops, and read industry publications to stay informed about the latest trends and best practices.

4: Building Credibility and Reputation

Importance: A strong network enhances an entrepreneur's credibility and reputation within their industry, making it easier to attract customers, investors, and partners.

Methods: Actively participate in industry events, contribute to discussions, and share expertise through speaking engagements, articles, and social media.

Effective Networking Strategies

1: Attending Industry Events

Importance: Industry events such as conferences, trade shows, and seminars provide opportunities to meet potential collaborators and learn about the latest trends.

Tips:

Prepare: Research attendees and speakers beforehand. Prepare a brief introduction and business cards.

Engage: Participate in sessions, ask questions, and introduce yourself to other attendees.

Follow Up: After the event, follow up with new contacts through email or LinkedIn to maintain the connection.

2: Joining Professional Associations

Importance: Professional associations offer networking opportunities, resources, and support for entrepreneurs within specific industries.

Tips:

Membership: Join relevant associations and actively participate in their events and activities.

Involvement: Volunteer for committees or leadership roles to increase visibility and build relationships.

3: Leveraging Online Platforms

Importance: Online platforms such as LinkedIn, Twitter, and industry-specific forums allow entrepreneurs to connect with a global network of professionals.

Tips:

Profile: Maintain a professional and updated online profile.

Engagement: Share valuable content, participate in discussions, and connect with industry leaders.

Groups: Join and actively participate in relevant online groups and communities.

4: Utilizing Local Networking Opportunities

Importance: Local networking groups, chambers of commerce, and business incubators provide opportunities to connect with nearby entrepreneurs and professionals.

Tips:

Meetups: Attend local meetups and networking events regularly.

Workspaces: Use co-working spaces to interact with other entrepreneurs and professionals.

The Importance of Collaboration

1: Combining Strengths and Resources

Importance: Collaboration allows entrepreneurs to leverage each other's strengths, skills, and resources, creating synergies that can lead to innovative solutions and business growth.

Methods: Identify complementary skills and resources among potential collaborators and establish clear roles and responsibilities.

Expanding Market Reach

Importance: Collaborating with others can help entrepreneurs access new markets, customer segments, and distribution channels.

Methods: Partner with businesses that have a strong presence in desired markets or complementary products and services.

2: Enhancing Creativity and Innovation

Importance: Collaboration fosters a creative environment where diverse ideas and perspectives can lead to breakthrough innovations.

Methods: Encourage open communication, brainstorming sessions, and cross-functional teams to stimulate creativity.

3: Sharing Risks and Rewards

Importance: Collaborative ventures allow entrepreneurs to share risks and rewards, reducing the individual burden and increasing the potential for success.

Methods: Establish clear agreements on profit-sharing, risk allocation, and decision-making processes.

Effective Collaboration Strategies

1: Building Trust and Rapport

Importance: Trust and rapport are the foundation of successful collaborations, ensuring open communication and mutual respect.

Tips:

Communication: Maintain transparent and consistent communication.

Reliability: Deliver on promises and meet deadlines.

Empathy: Understand and consider the perspectives and needs of collaborators.

1: Establishing Clear Goals and Expectations

Importance: Clear goals and expectations align collaborators towards a common objective, minimizing misunderstandings and conflicts.

Tips:

Objectives: Define clear, measurable goals for the collaboration.

Roles: Clearly outline roles, responsibilities, and expectations for each party.

Milestones: Set regular milestones and checkpoints to track progress.

2: Leveraging Technology for Collaboration

Importance: Technology facilitates efficient and effective collaboration, especially for remote or distributed teams.

Tips:

Tools: Use collaboration tools such as Slack, Trello, and Zoom for communication, project management, and virtual meetings.

Documents: Utilize cloud-based platforms like Google Drive and Dropbox for document sharing and collaboration.

3: Encouraging Open and Constructive Feedback

Importance: Open and constructive feedback fosters continuous improvement and innovation within collaborative ventures.

Tips:

Feedback: Regularly solicit and provide feedback.

Culture: Create a culture where feedback is viewed as an opportunity for growth, not criticism.

Improvements: Act on feedback to make necessary adjustments and improvements.

Case Study: The Founding of Instagram

Instagram's success story highlights the power of networking and collaboration. Founders Kevin Systrom and Mike Krieger met through mutual connections and shared their passion for technology and photography. Their collaboration combined Systrom's expertise in business and marketing with Krieger's skills in software engineering, leading to the creation of a highly successful social media platform.

By networking within the tech community and leveraging their complementary skills, Systrom and Krieger were able to develop, refine, and launch Instagram. Their collaborative approach allowed them to innovate rapidly, respond to user feedback, and ultimately achieve significant success.

Conclusion

Networking and collaboration are essential for entrepreneurial success. By building a strong network, entrepreneurs can access diverse perspectives, learn from others, and discover new opportunities. Effective collaboration leverages the strengths and resources of multiple parties, fostering innovation and enhancing business growth. Entrepreneurs should actively engage in networking and seek out collaborative opportunities, building relationships that drive their ventures forward. Through strategic networking and collaboration, entrepreneurs can unlock their full potential and create impactful, successful businesses.

Chapter 8
Customer Feedback and Insights

The Value of Customer Feedback

Customer feedback is a powerful tool for entrepreneurs. It provides direct insights into customer needs, preferences, and pain points, enabling entrepreneurs to generate ideas that truly resonate with their target market. This chapter explores how to gather, interpret, and leverage customer feedback to drive innovation and create solutions that meet customer demands.

Gathering Customer Feedback

1: Conducting Surveys

Importance: Surveys are an effective way to collect quantitative data from a large sample of customers. They help entrepreneurs understand general trends, preferences, and opinions.

Methods:

Designing Surveys: Create clear, concise questions that address specific aspects of the product or service. Use a mix of multiple-choice, rating scale, and open-ended questions.

Distributing Surveys: Use online survey tools like SurveyMonkey, Google Forms, or Typeform to reach a wide audience. Promote surveys through email newsletters, social media, and website pop-ups.

Analyzing Survey Data: Use statistical analysis tools to identify patterns, trends, and key insights from survey responses.

2: Organizing Focus Groups

Importance: Focus groups provide in-depth qualitative insights through guided discussions with a small group of participants. They help uncover detailed feedback, emotions, and motivations.

Methods:

Selecting Participants: Choose a diverse group of participants that represents the target market. Aim for 6-12 participants per session.

Facilitating Discussions: Prepare a discussion guide with open-ended questions. Encourage participants to share their thoughts freely and interact with each other.

Recording and Analyzing: Record the sessions (with permission) and transcribe the discussions. Analyze the transcripts for recurring themes, insights, and suggestions.

3: Gathering Online Reviews

Importance: Online reviews offer a wealth of unsolicited feedback from customers. They provide real-world insights into customer experiences and perceptions.

Methods:

Monitoring Review Platforms: Regularly monitor review sites such as Yelp, Google Reviews, and Amazon. Use tools like ReviewTrackers or Trustpilot to aggregate reviews from multiple platforms.

Analyzing Reviews: Categorize reviews into positive, negative, and neutral. Identify common themes, praises, and complaints. Pay attention to detailed reviews that provide specific feedback.

Responding to Reviews: Engage with reviewers by acknowledging their feedback and addressing their concerns. This shows that the business values customer input and is committed to improvement.

4: Utilizing Social Media

Importance: Social media platforms provide a direct channel for customers to share their opinions and experiences. They offer real-time feedback and a pulse on customer sentiment.

Methods:

Social Listening: Use social listening tools like Hootsuite, Sprout Social, or Brandwatch to track mentions, hashtags, and discussions related to the brand or industry.

Engaging with Followers: Actively engage with followers by responding to comments, messages, and mentions. Conduct polls and ask questions to solicit feedback.

Analyzing Social Data: Analyze social media data to identify trends, popular topics, and areas of improvement. Use sentiment analysis tools to gauge overall customer sentiment.

Interpreting Customer Feedback

1: Identifying Key Insights

Importance: Identifying key insights from customer feedback helps entrepreneurs focus on the most relevant and impactful information.

Methods:

Thematic Analysis: Group similar feedback into themes or categories. Look for patterns and commonalities that indicate underlying issues or opportunities.

Prioritizing Feedback: Prioritize feedback based on frequency, severity, and potential impact. Focus on issues that affect a large portion of customers or significantly impact their experience.

2: Understanding Customer Needs and Pain Points

Importance: Understanding customer needs and pain points allows entrepreneurs to develop solutions that address real problems and enhance customer satisfaction.

Methods:

Customer Journey Mapping: Map out the customer journey to identify pain points and areas for improvement. Consider all touchpoints, from initial awareness to post-purchase support.

Empathy Mapping: Create empathy maps to understand customers' emotions, thoughts, and behaviors. This helps in designing solutions that resonate with their experiences.

3: Validating Ideas with Customers

Importance: Validating ideas with customers ensures that proposed solutions align with their needs and expectations.

Methods:

Prototyping and Testing: Develop prototypes or mockups of new ideas and test them with a small group of customers. Gather feedback on usability, functionality, and overall appeal.

A/B Testing: Conduct A/B tests to compare different versions of a product, feature, or marketing message. Use customer feedback and data to determine which version performs better.

Leveraging Customer Feedback for Idea Generation

1: Incorporating Feedback into Product Development

Importance: Incorporating customer feedback into product development ensures that new products or features meet customer needs and preferences.

Methods:

Agile Development: Use agile development methodologies to iterate on products based on customer feedback. Regularly release updates and improvements.

Customer Advisory Boards: Establish customer advisory boards to gather ongoing feedback and input on product development. Involve key customers in the design and testing phases.

2: Enhancing Customer Experience

Importance: Improving customer experience based on feedback can lead to increased satisfaction, loyalty, and positive word-of-mouth.

Methods:

Personalization: Use customer data to personalize experiences, products, and communications. Tailor offerings to individual preferences and behaviors.

Customer Support Improvements: Enhance customer support based on feedback. Implement new channels, reduce response times, and improve the quality of service.

3: Innovating Based on Customer Insights

Importance: Customer insights can inspire new business ideas, products, or services that address unmet needs and create value.

Methods:

Idea Workshops: Conduct idea workshops with cross-functional teams to brainstorm solutions based on customer insights. Use techniques like mind mapping and design thinking.

Co-Creation: Involve customers in the innovation process through co-creation initiatives. Collaborate with customers to design new products, services, or features.

Case Study: Slack

Slack, the popular team collaboration tool, exemplifies the effective use of customer feedback for product development and innovation. Initially developed as an internal communication tool for a gaming company, Slack's founders realized its potential as a standalone product based on feedback from early users.

Throughout its development, Slack consistently gathered and analyzed customer feedback through surveys, focus groups, and social media. They identified pain points in existing communication tools, such as poor integration, limited functionality, and lack of user-friendliness. By addressing these issues and incorporating user suggestions, Slack created a product that resonated with a wide range of users.

Slack's continuous improvement and innovation, driven by customer insights, have contributed to its success as a leading communication platform used by millions of teams worldwide.

Conclusion

Customer feedback and insights are invaluable for generating ideas that meet real needs and drive business success. By effectively gathering and interpreting feedback through surveys, focus groups, online reviews, and social media, entrepreneurs can gain a deep understanding of customer preferences and pain points. Leveraging these insights to guide product development, enhance customer experience, and inspire innovation ensures that businesses stay relevant, competitive, and customer-centric. Entrepreneurs should prioritize customer feedback as a key component of their idea generation and business strategy, continuously seeking ways to improve and innovate based on customer needs.

Chapter 9
Creative Thinking Techniques

The Power of Creative Thinking

Creative thinking is essential for entrepreneurs seeking to unlock new perspectives and generate innovative ideas. It involves looking at problems and opportunities from different angles and breaking free from conventional thinking patterns. This chapter introduces various creative thinking techniques, including lateral thinking, reverse brainstorming, and the six thinking hats method, to enhance the entrepreneurial idea generation process.

Lateral Thinking

1: Understanding Lateral Thinking

Importance: Lateral thinking involves solving problems through an indirect and creative approach, often by viewing the problem in a new and unconventional light.

Concept: Coined by Edward de Bono, lateral thinking encourages the generation of ideas that are not immediately obvious and that break away from traditional step-by-step reasoning.

2: Techniques for Lateral Thinking

Random Input: Introduce a random word or concept and see how it relates to the problem at hand. This can lead to unexpected connections and ideas.

Example: If you're trying to innovate in the transportation industry, randomly choose the word "butterfly" and explore how its characteristics (e.g., lightness, metamorphosis) could inspire new solutions.

Provocative Statements: Make seemingly absurd or provocative statements to challenge assumptions and stimulate creative thinking.

Example: "What if cars could float?" This can lead to brainstorming about new forms of transportation, such as amphibious vehicles or anti-gravity technology.

Concept Fan: Start with a broad concept and expand it into more specific ideas by creating a concept fan. This helps in exploring different facets and possibilities of the main idea.

Example: Start with "improving public transportation" and branch out to specific ideas like "electric buses," "bike-sharing programs," or "on-demand shuttle services."

Reverse Brainstorming

1: Understanding Reverse Brainstorming

Importance: Reverse brainstorming involves identifying ways to make a problem worse, which can then be flipped to find solutions for improving the situation. It helps in identifying potential pitfalls and areas for innovation.

Concept: Instead of asking how to solve a problem, ask how to create or exacerbate it, then reverse those ideas to find solutions.

2: Steps for Reverse Brainstorming

Define the Problem: Clearly define the problem you want to solve.

Example: "How can we improve customer satisfaction in our restaurant?"

Reverse the Problem: Ask how to make the problem worse.

Example: "How can we decrease customer satisfaction in our restaurant?"

Generate Reverse Ideas: Brainstorm ideas on how to achieve the reversed problem.

Example: "Serve cold food," "Ignore customer complaints," "Have long wait times."

Flip the Ideas: Reverse the negative ideas to find potential solutions.

Example: "Serve hot and fresh food," "Address customer complaints promptly," "Reduce wait times."

3: Benefits of Reverse Brainstorming

Identifying Weaknesses: Helps in identifying weaknesses and areas for improvement that might not be immediately obvious.

Stimulating Creativity: Encourages thinking outside the box and considering unconventional solutions.

The Six Thinking Hats Method

1: Understanding the Six Thinking Hats

Importance: The Six Thinking Hats method, developed by Edward de Bono, encourages parallel thinking and helps individuals and teams explore different perspectives systematically.

Concept: Each "hat" represents a different mode of thinking, allowing for a comprehensive examination of ideas and problems.

2: The Six Hats and Their Roles

White Hat (Facts and Information): Focuses on data, facts, and objective information.

Example: "What data do we have about customer preferences?"

Red Hat (Emotions and Feelings): Considers emotional responses, intuitions, and gut feelings.

Example: "How do we feel about this idea? What are our gut reactions?"

Black Hat (Caution and Criticism): Identifies potential problems, risks, and challenges.

Example: "What are the potential downsides or risks of this idea?"

Yellow Hat (Optimism and Benefits): Looks at the positive aspects and benefits of an idea.

Example: "What are the advantages and benefits of this idea?"

Green Hat (Creativity and Alternatives): Encourages creative thinking and exploring alternative solutions.

Example: "What are some creative alternatives to this idea?"

Blue Hat (Process and Control): Focuses on managing the thinking process and ensuring that all perspectives are considered.

Example: "What is our objective? What should we think about next?"

3: Using the Six Thinking Hats in Practice

Structured Discussion: Assign each hat to different team members or switch hats sequentially to explore all aspects of a problem.

Balanced Perspective: Ensures a balanced perspective by considering facts, emotions, risks, benefits, creativity, and process management.

Enhanced Collaboration: Promotes collaborative thinking and reduces conflicts by separating different types of thinking.

Implementing Creative Thinking Techniques

1: Creating a Creative Environment

Importance: A supportive environment fosters creativity and encourages innovative thinking.

Methods:

Physical Space: Design a workspace that stimulates creativity with open spaces, comfortable seating, and inspiring decor.

Psychological Safety: Encourage an open-minded culture where all ideas are valued, and there is no fear of criticism.

2: Encouraging Team Participation

Importance: Diverse perspectives lead to richer ideas and solutions.

Methods:

Inclusivity: Involve team members from different departments and backgrounds in brainstorming sessions.

Facilitation: Use skilled facilitators to guide creative thinking sessions and ensure productive discussions.

3: Using Technology to Enhance Creativity

Importance: Technology can provide tools and platforms that enhance the creative process.

Methods:

Digital Collaboration Tools: Use tools like Miro, Trello, or Slack for virtual brainstorming and collaboration.

Idea Management Software: Implement software like IdeaScale or MindMeister to capture, organize, and prioritize ideas.

Case Study: IDEO

IDEO, a global design and innovation firm, is renowned for its creative thinking techniques and innovative solutions. The company employs a variety of methods, including lateral thinking, reverse brainstorming, and the Six Thinking Hats, to develop groundbreaking products and services for clients across various industries.

IDEO's collaborative and human-centered approach involves deep user research, iterative prototyping, and continuous feedback. By fostering a culture of creativity and leveraging diverse perspectives, IDEO consistently delivers innovative solutions that meet user needs and drive business success.

Conclusion

Creative thinking is a critical skill for entrepreneurs seeking to generate innovative ideas and solutions. Techniques such as lateral thinking, reverse brainstorming, and the Six Thinking Hats method provide structured approaches to break free from conventional thinking patterns and explore new perspectives. By creating a supportive environment, encouraging team participation, and leveraging technology, entrepreneurs can enhance their creative thinking capabilities and drive business innovation. Embracing these techniques will help entrepreneurs develop unique, impactful ideas that address real-world problems and create value for their customers and stakeholders.

Chapter 10
Innovation and Disruption

Understanding Innovation and Disruption

Innovation is the process of creating new products, services, or processes that bring significant value to customers and businesses. Disruption, a term popularized by Harvard Business School professor Clayton Christensen, refers to innovations that significantly alter or completely transform existing markets or industries, often displacing established market leaders. This chapter delves into the concept of disruptive innovation and provides guidance on how entrepreneurs can generate ideas that challenge the status quo and create new markets.

The Concept of Disruptive Innovation

1: Definition of Disruptive Innovation

Importance: Disruptive innovation redefines how markets operate, offering simpler, cheaper, or more accessible solutions that cater to underserved or entirely new customer segments.

Characteristics:

Simpler and Cheaper: Disruptive innovations often start as simpler, more affordable alternatives to existing solutions.

New Market Creation: They create new markets or significantly alter existing ones by addressing unmet needs.

Initial Inferiority: These innovations may initially perform worse than existing products in some aspects but improve over time.

2: Types of Disruptive Innovation

Low-End Disruption: Targets customers who are overserved by existing solutions, offering a simpler and cheaper alternative.

Example: Southwest Airlines disrupted the airline industry by offering low-cost, no-frills flights.

New-Market Disruption: Targets non-consumers or new customer segments who were previously unable to access the market due to cost or complexity.

Example: The personal computer disrupted the mainframe computer industry by making computing accessible to individuals and small businesses.

Generating Disruptive Ideas

Identifying Market Gaps and Pain Points

Importance: Disruptive ideas often arise from identifying significant gaps or pain points in the market that existing solutions fail to address.

Methods:

Customer Feedback: Gather and analyze customer feedback to identify unmet needs and frustrations.

Market Research: Conduct thorough market research to uncover underserved or overlooked segments.

Competitive Analysis: Study competitors to identify weaknesses or gaps in their offerings.

1: Embracing Technological Advancements

Importance: Technological advancements can enable the development of disruptive solutions that were previously not possible.

Methods:

Stay Informed: Keep abreast of emerging technologies and trends in your industry.

Experimentation: Invest in research and development to explore how new technologies can be applied to create innovative solutions.

Collaboration: Partner with tech companies, startups, or research institutions to leverage their expertise and resources.

2: Leveraging Business Model Innovation

Importance: Sometimes, disruption comes not from the product itself but from a novel business model that changes how value is delivered and captured.

Methods:

Subscription Models: Explore subscription-based models that offer continuous value and convenience.

Freemium Models: Offer a basic version of the product for free while charging for premium features or services.

Platform Models: Develop platforms that connect different user groups, creating network effects and new value propositions.

3: Cultivating a Disruptive Mindset

Importance: A disruptive mindset involves questioning assumptions, embracing risk, and thinking unconventionally.

Methods:

Question Assumptions: Regularly challenge existing assumptions about your industry, customers, and products.

Risk-Taking: Encourage calculated risk-taking and experimentation within your team.

Unconventional Thinking: Foster a culture that values creative and unconventional ideas.

Implementing Disruptive Innovations

1: Prototyping and Testing

Importance: Prototyping and testing allow you to validate disruptive ideas quickly and efficiently.

Methods:

Rapid Prototyping: Develop quick, low-cost prototypes to test key features and concepts.

User Testing: Conduct user testing sessions to gather feedback and iterate on the design.

Pilot Programs: Launch pilot programs to test the innovation in a real-world setting with a small group of users.

2: Scaling and Market Entry

Importance: Successfully scaling and entering the market are critical for turning disruptive ideas into profitable ventures.

Methods:

Phased Rollout: Implement a phased rollout strategy to manage risk and gather feedback at each stage.

Marketing and Positioning: Develop a compelling marketing strategy that highlights the unique value proposition of the disruptive innovation.

Distribution Channels: Identify and leverage effective distribution channels to reach your target market.

3: Overcoming Resistance

Importance: Disruptive innovations often face resistance from incumbents and established market players.

Methods:

Stakeholder Engagement: Engage key stakeholders early to build support and mitigate resistance.

Education and Communication: Educate the market about the benefits and value of the innovation through clear and consistent communication.

Persistence and Adaptability: Be persistent in your efforts and adaptable in responding to challenges and resistance.

Case Study: Netflix

Netflix is a prime example of disruptive innovation. Initially, Netflix disrupted the video rental industry by offering a subscription-based DVD rental service through mail, providing greater convenience and selection than traditional rental stores like Blockbuster. As technology advanced, Netflix embraced streaming technology, further disrupting the entertainment industry by providing on-demand streaming services. This innovation not only changed how people consume media but also challenged traditional cable and satellite TV providers.

By continuously identifying market gaps, leveraging technological advancements, and adopting innovative business models, Netflix successfully disrupted multiple industries and established itself as a market leader.

Conclusion

Disruptive innovation is a powerful force that can transform industries, create new markets, and drive significant growth. Entrepreneurs who understand the principles of disruptive innovation and actively seek to identify market gaps, leverage technology, and innovate business models can generate ideas that challenge the status quo. By cultivating a disruptive mindset, prototyping and testing ideas, and effectively scaling and entering the market, entrepreneurs can turn disruptive ideas into successful ventures. Embracing innovation and disruption will enable entrepreneurs to stay ahead of the competition and create lasting value for their customers and stakeholders.

Chapter 11
Cross-Industry Innovation

The Concept of Cross-Industry Innovation

Cross-industry innovation involves borrowing and adapting ideas, processes, and technologies from one industry to another. This approach can lead to breakthrough solutions and novel business models by applying successful concepts from different fields. This chapter explores how entrepreneurs can leverage cross-industry innovation to generate unique and effective ideas for their own businesses.

The Importance of Cross-Industry Innovation

1: Expanding Perspectives

Importance: Looking beyond one's own industry broadens perspectives and fosters creative thinking.

Benefits: Exposure to diverse practices and solutions can spark new ideas and challenge conventional thinking.

2: Accelerating Innovation

Importance: Cross-industry innovation can accelerate the innovation process by leveraging existing solutions.

Benefits: Instead of reinventing the wheel, entrepreneurs can adapt proven concepts to their own industry, saving time and resources.

3: Creating Competitive Advantage

Importance: Applying ideas from other industries can differentiate a business from its competitors.

Benefits: Unique adaptations can lead to a competitive edge, attracting customers and increasing market share.

Steps to Implement Cross-Industry Innovation

1: Identifying Relevant Industries

Importance: Choosing the right industries to explore is crucial for finding applicable and valuable ideas.

Methods:

Similarity in Challenges: Look for industries facing similar challenges or serving similar customer needs.

Technological Parallels: Identify industries with advanced technologies that can be adapted to your own.

Business Model Analogies: Consider industries with business models that can be reinterpreted for your market.

2: Conducting Research

Importance: Thorough research is essential to understand how successful concepts from other industries can be adapted.

Methods:

Case Studies: Study case studies and success stories from other industries to identify key factors and practices.

Industry Reports: Read industry reports and whitepapers to gain insights into trends, innovations, and best practices.

Expert Interviews: Conduct interviews with experts from other fields to gain deeper understanding and practical insights.

3: Adapting and Testing Ideas

Importance: Ideas from other industries need to be adapted to fit the specific context and needs of your business.

Methods:

Conceptual Adaptation: Modify concepts to align with your industry's unique characteristics and requirements.

Prototyping: Develop prototypes to test the adapted ideas in a controlled environment.

Pilot Programs: Implement pilot programs to test the ideas on a small scale before full-scale deployment.

Examples of Cross-Industry Innovation

1: Healthcare and Hospitality

Example: The Cleveland Clinic applied principles from the hospitality industry to improve patient experience. By adopting customer service practices from luxury hotels, they enhanced patient satisfaction and care quality.

2: Retail and Entertainment

Example: Apple Stores revolutionized retail by incorporating elements from entertainment and theme parks. The focus on immersive experiences and interactive displays created a unique and engaging shopping environment.

3: Automotive and Technology

Example: Tesla borrowed ideas from the technology sector, particularly in software development and user interfaces, to create a new kind of automotive experience. The integration of advanced software features and over-the-air updates set Tesla apart in the auto industry.

Strategies for Successful Cross-Industry Innovation

1: Fostering a Culture of Curiosity

Importance: A culture of curiosity encourages team members to explore and experiment with ideas from various fields.

Methods:

Continuous Learning: Promote continuous learning and knowledge sharing through workshops, seminars, and industry conferences.

Encouraging Exploration: Allow time and resources for employees to explore and experiment with ideas from different industries.

2: Building Diverse Teams

Importance: Diverse teams bring varied perspectives and experiences, enhancing the potential for cross-industry innovation.

Methods:

Hiring Practices: Hire individuals with backgrounds in different industries and disciplines.

Interdisciplinary Collaboration: Foster interdisciplinary collaboration by creating cross-functional teams and encouraging knowledge exchange.

3: Creating Strategic Partnerships

Importance: Partnerships with companies from other industries can provide valuable insights and resources.

Methods:

Collaborative Projects: Engage in collaborative projects with firms from different sectors to co-develop innovative solutions.

Knowledge Exchange Programs: Establish knowledge exchange programs to facilitate the sharing of best practices and innovations.

Tools and Techniques for Cross-Industry Innovation

1: Trend Analysis

Importance: Identifying trends in other industries can inspire new ideas and adaptations.

Methods:

Trend Reports: Subscribe to trend reports and newsletters from various industries.

Trend Watching: Use trend-watching platforms like TrendWatching or TrendHunter to stay informed about emerging trends.

2: Analogous Thinking

Importance: Analogous thinking involves drawing parallels between seemingly unrelated fields to generate new ideas.

Methods:

Analogy Mapping: Create analogy maps to visually explore connections between different industries and concepts.

Scenario Planning: Use scenario planning to envision how ideas from other industries could be applied to your business.

3: Innovation Labs

Importance: Innovation labs provide a dedicated space for experimentation and collaboration.

Methods:

Establishing Labs: Set up innovation labs within your organization to facilitate cross-industry exploration and prototyping.

Collaborative Spaces: Create collaborative spaces that encourage interaction and idea sharing among team members from different disciplines.

Case Study: Airbnb

Airbnb is a prime example of cross-industry innovation. The founders drew inspiration from various industries to create a unique business model. They combined elements of hospitality, real estate, and the sharing economy to develop a platform that allows individuals to rent out their homes or spare rooms to travelers. This cross-industry approach disrupted the traditional hotel industry and created a new market for peer-to-peer lodging.

Conclusion

Cross-industry innovation is a powerful strategy for generating unique and effective business ideas. By looking beyond their own field and adapting successful concepts from other industries, entrepreneurs can expand their perspectives, accelerate innovation, and create a competitive advantage. Through identifying relevant industries, conducting thorough research, and fostering a culture of curiosity, entrepreneurs can successfully implement cross-industry innovations.

Embracing diverse teams, strategic partnerships, and tools like trend analysis and innovation labs will further enhance the potential for breakthrough ideas and transformative solutions.

Chapter 12
Using Technology for Idea Generation

The Role of Technology in Idea Generation

Technology has revolutionized the way entrepreneurs generate and refine ideas. By leveraging advanced tools and platforms, entrepreneurs can streamline the ideation process, uncover new insights, and enhance their creativity. This chapter explores various technological solutions that facilitate idea generation, including artificial intelligence (AI), data analytics, and innovation management software.

The Impact of Technology on Innovation

1: Enhanced Creativity and Efficiency

Importance: Technology enhances both the creative and operational aspects of idea generation.

Benefits: Streamlined processes and enhanced capabilities allow for faster, more effective ideation and problem-solving.

2: Data-Driven Insights

Importance: Data analytics provides actionable insights that can guide the ideation process.

Benefits: Entrepreneurs can make informed decisions and identify opportunities based on real-world data.

3: Collaboration and Communication

Importance: Technology facilitates collaboration and communication among teams, stakeholders, and external partners.

Benefits: Enhanced collaboration leads to richer ideas and more innovative solutions.

Tools and Platforms for Idea Generation

1: Artificial Intelligence (AI)

Role in Idea Generation: AI can automate the ideation process, analyze large datasets, and provide creative solutions.

Applications:

AI-Powered Brainstorming: Tools like Ideanote and Notion AI use AI to generate and organize ideas based on specific prompts.

Pattern Recognition: AI algorithms identify patterns and trends in data, revealing opportunities and insights.

Natural Language Processing (NLP): NLP tools analyze text data, such as customer reviews and market research reports, to uncover hidden insights and ideas.

2: Data Analytics

Role in Idea Generation: Data analytics tools process and analyze data to generate actionable insights and identify trends.

Applications:

Customer Insights: Platforms like Google Analytics and Tableau analyze customer behavior and preferences, helping entrepreneurs identify unmet needs.

Market Trends: Tools like Trendalyzer and Statista provide data on market trends and industry dynamics, guiding strategic decision-making.

Competitive Analysis: Software like SEMrush and Ahrefs analyze competitors' activities, revealing opportunities for differentiation and innovation.

3: Innovation Management Software

Role in Idea Generation: Innovation management software helps manage the entire ideation process, from idea capture to evaluation and implementation.

Applications:

Idea Capture: Tools like Brightidea and IdeaScale allow teams to submit and organize ideas in a centralized platform.

Collaboration: Platforms like Spigit and Wazoku facilitate collaboration and discussion around ideas, fostering a culture of innovation.

Evaluation and Prioritization: Software like Planbox and HYPE Innovation provide frameworks for evaluating and prioritizing ideas based on criteria such as feasibility, impact, and alignment with business goals.

Implementing Technology for Idea Generation

1: Choosing the Right Tools

Importance: Selecting the right tools is crucial for effectively leveraging technology in the ideation process.

Methods:

Needs Assessment: Conduct a thorough needs assessment to identify the specific requirements and goals of your ideation process.

Feature Evaluation: Evaluate the features and capabilities of various tools to ensure they align with your needs.

User Experience: Consider the user experience and ease of use to ensure that the tools are accessible and intuitive for your team.

2: Integrating Technology into the Workflow

Importance: Seamlessly integrating technology into your workflow enhances its effectiveness and ensures its adoption.

Methods:

Process Mapping: Map out your current ideation process and identify areas where technology can be integrated.

Training and Support: Provide training and support to ensure that team members are comfortable using the new tools.

Continuous Improvement: Continuously monitor and refine the integration of technology to ensure it meets evolving needs and goals.

3: Encouraging a Tech-Driven Culture

Importance: A tech-driven culture encourages the adoption and effective use of technology for idea generation.

Methods:

Leadership Support: Ensure that leadership supports and champions the use of technology for ideation.

Incentives: Offer incentives and recognition for team members who effectively use technology to generate innovative ideas.

Feedback Loop: Establish a feedback loop to gather input from team members on the effectiveness of the tools and make necessary adjustments.

Case Studies: Technology-Driven Idea Generation

1: Amazon and AI-Powered Innovation

Example: Amazon uses AI extensively to drive innovation across its business. The company leverages AI for product recommendations, inventory management, and customer service, continually generating new ideas to enhance customer experience and operational efficiency.

2: Procter & Gamble and Data Analytics

Example: Procter & Gamble (P&G) uses data analytics to drive its innovation strategy. By analyzing consumer data, market trends, and competitor activities, P&G identifies opportunities for new product development and market expansion, ensuring that its innovations are data-driven and customer-focused.

3: Google and Innovation Management Software

Example: Google uses innovation management software to capture and evaluate ideas from employees across the organization. The company's internal platform allows team members to submit ideas, collaborate on solutions, and prioritize initiatives based on their potential impact and feasibility.

Conclusion

Technology is a powerful enabler of idea generation for entrepreneurs. By leveraging tools and platforms such as AI, data analytics, and innovation management software, entrepreneurs can enhance their creativity, uncover valuable insights, and streamline the ideation process. Implementing the right technology, integrating it into the workflow, and fostering a tech-driven culture are essential for maximizing the benefits of technology in idea generation. Through case studies and practical applications, this chapter demonstrates how technology can transform the way entrepreneurs generate and refine ideas, driving innovation and business success.

Chapter 13
Idea Validation and Feasibility

The Importance of Idea Validation and Feasibility

Not all ideas, no matter how creative or innovative, are worth pursuing. Validating and assessing the feasibility of ideas is a critical step in the entrepreneurial process to ensure that resources are invested wisely. This chapter guides entrepreneurs through the process of validating and assessing the feasibility of their ideas, including market testing, prototyping, and financial analysis.

Understanding Idea Validation

1: Definition of Idea Validation

Importance: Idea validation involves evaluating whether an idea has the potential to succeed in the market.

Benefits: Reduces the risk of failure, saves time and resources, and provides insights into the market needs and preferences.

2: Stages of Idea Validation

Concept Validation: Assessing the initial idea concept to ensure it addresses a real problem or need.

Market Validation: Testing the idea with potential customers to gauge interest and demand.

Technical Validation: Ensuring the idea is technically feasible and can be developed within the available resources.

Business Validation: Evaluating the idea's business model and financial viability.

Methods of Idea Validation

1: Market Research

Importance: Market research helps understand the target audience, their needs, and the competitive landscape.

Methods:

Surveys and Questionnaires: Collect data from potential customers about their preferences and pain points.

Interviews and Focus Groups: Engage directly with potential users to gain deeper insights into their needs and reactions to the idea.

Competitive Analysis: Study competitors to understand their offerings, strengths, and weaknesses.

2: Prototyping

Importance: Prototyping involves creating a preliminary model of the product or service to test its functionality and appeal.

Methods:

Low-Fidelity Prototypes: Simple models such as sketches, wireframes, or mock-ups to visualize the idea.

High-Fidelity Prototypes: More detailed and functional prototypes that closely resemble the final product.

User Testing: Testing prototypes with potential users to gather feedback and identify areas for improvement.

3: Minimum Viable Product (MVP)

Importance: An MVP is a simplified version of the product that includes only the core features necessary to test the idea in the market.

Methods:

Feature Selection: Identify and develop the essential features that solve the primary problem or need.

Launch and Test: Release the MVP to a small group of users and collect feedback on its usability and value.

Iterate and Improve: Use the feedback to refine and enhance the product before a full-scale launch.

Assessing Feasibility

1: Technical Feasibility

Importance: Evaluating whether the idea can be developed with the available technology and resources.

Methods:

Technical Assessment: Review the technical requirements and challenges associated with the idea.

Resource Evaluation: Assess the availability of necessary resources, including skills, tools, and infrastructure.

Prototype Development: Create a technical prototype to test the feasibility and identify potential issues.

2: Market Feasibility

Importance: Determining if there is a sufficient market demand for the idea.

Methods:

Market Size Analysis: Estimate the size of the target market and its growth potential.

Customer Segmentation: Identify and analyze different customer segments to understand their specific needs and preferences.

Competitive Positioning: Assess how the idea compares to existing solutions in the market and identify unique selling points.

3: Financial Feasibility

Importance: Ensuring the idea is financially viable and can generate a sustainable return on investment.

Methods:

Cost Analysis: Estimate the costs associated with developing, marketing, and scaling the idea.

Revenue Projections: Forecast potential revenue streams based on market research and pricing strategies.

Break-Even Analysis: Calculate the break-even point to determine how long it will take to recover the initial investment.

Financial Models: Develop financial models to simulate different scenarios and assess the financial viability of the idea.

Practical Steps for Idea Validation and Feasibility

1: Define Objectives and Metrics

Importance: Clear objectives and metrics help measure the success of the validation process.

Methods:

Objective Setting: Define what you aim to achieve with the validation process, such as understanding market demand or assessing technical feasibility.

Key Metrics: Identify key metrics to track, such as customer interest, prototype functionality, and financial projections.

2: Develop a Validation Plan

Importance: A structured plan ensures a systematic approach to idea validation and feasibility assessment.

Methods:

Step-by-Step Plan: Outline the steps involved in the validation process, including market research, prototyping, and financial analysis.

Timeline and Milestones: Establish a timeline with specific milestones to track progress and make adjustments as needed.

3: Execute and Iterate

Importance: Execution and iteration are crucial for refining the idea based on feedback and findings.

Methods:

Implementation: Execute the validation plan, gathering data and feedback at each stage.

Iteration: Continuously refine the idea based on insights and feedback, making necessary adjustments to improve feasibility.

Case Study: Dropbox

Dropbox provides a compelling example of effective idea validation and feasibility assessment. The founders created a simple video demonstrating the concept of Dropbox, showcasing how it would solve common file-sharing problems. This video was shared on various platforms, and the positive response from potential users validated the demand for the product. Based on this feedback, the founders developed a prototype (MVP) and continued to iterate and improve the product, ultimately leading to its successful launch and growth.

Conclusion

Idea validation and feasibility assessment are crucial steps in the entrepreneurial process, ensuring that only viable and valuable ideas are pursued. By employing methods such as market research, prototyping, and financial analysis, entrepreneurs can effectively evaluate their ideas and make informed decisions. Implementing a structured validation plan, defining clear objectives and metrics, and embracing a cycle of execution and iteration will enhance the likelihood of success. Through practical examples and detailed guidance, this chapter equips entrepreneurs with the tools and knowledge needed to validate and assess the feasibility of their ideas, paving the way for successful innovation and business growth.

Chapter 14
Developing a Value Proposition

The Importance of a Value Proposition

A value proposition is a clear statement that explains how your product or service solves a customer's problem or improves their situation, delivers specific benefits, and tells the ideal customer why they should buy from you and not from the competition. A strong value proposition is essential for any business idea as it is the foundation for marketing strategies and customer engagement. This chapter explores how to craft a compelling value proposition that clearly communicates the benefits of your idea to potential customers.

Understanding the Value Proposition

1: Definition of a Value Proposition

Importance: A value proposition articulates the unique value your product or service provides.

Benefits: It differentiates your offering from competitors and convinces potential customers of its worth.

2: Components of a Value Proposition

Target Audience: Identify who your ideal customers are.

Problem Statement: Define the specific problem your product or service addresses.

Solution: Describe how your product or service solves the problem.

Benefits: Highlight the key benefits and outcomes customers can expect.

Unique Selling Points (USPs): Explain what makes your solution different and better than others.

Crafting a Compelling Value Proposition

1: Identify Your Target Audience

Importance: Understanding your audience is crucial for tailoring your value proposition.

Methods:

Customer Segmentation: Divide your market into distinct groups based on demographics, behaviors, and needs.

Buyer Personas: Create detailed profiles of your ideal customers to better understand their motivations and challenges.

2: Define the Problem

Importance: Clearly defining the problem ensures that your value proposition addresses a real need.

Methods:

Market Research: Use surveys, interviews, and focus groups to gather insights into the problems faced by your target audience.

Customer Feedback: Analyze feedback from current or potential customers to identify common pain points.

3: Describe Your Solution

Importance: Your solution should directly address the problem you've identified.

Methods:

Feature-Benefit Mapping: Map out the features of your product or service and link them to the benefits they provide.

Clear and Concise Messaging: Ensure your description is straightforward and easy to understand.

4: Highlight the Benefits

Importance: Benefits show customers the tangible outcomes of using your product or service.

Methods:

Value Mapping: Create a value map to visualize how your solution delivers specific benefits.

Quantify Benefits: Where possible, use data and metrics to quantify the benefits (e.g., time saved, cost reduced).

5: Differentiate Your Offering

Importance: Differentiation is key to standing out in a competitive market.

Methods:

Competitive Analysis: Study competitors to understand their value propositions and identify gaps or opportunities.

Unique Selling Points (USPs): Focus on what makes your product or service unique and superior.

Communicating Your Value Proposition

1: Creating an Elevator Pitch

Importance: An elevator pitch is a brief and persuasive summary of your value proposition.

Methods:

Concise Statement: Craft a statement that can be delivered in 30-60 seconds, clearly articulating the problem, solution, and benefits.

Practice and Refine: Continuously practice and refine your pitch to ensure it is compelling and memorable.

2: Developing Marketing Messages

Importance: Consistent and clear marketing messages help communicate your value proposition to your audience.

Methods:

Taglines and Slogans: Create memorable taglines and slogans that encapsulate your value proposition.

Content Marketing: Use blogs, social media, and other content to elaborate on and reinforce your value proposition.

3: Visual Representation

Importance: Visuals can enhance the communication of your value proposition.

Methods:

Infographics: Use infographics to visually represent the problem, solution, and benefits.

Videos: Create explainer videos that detail your value proposition in an engaging format.

Testing and Refining Your Value Proposition

1: Customer Feedback

Importance: Feedback helps refine and improve your value proposition.

Methods:

Surveys and Interviews: Conduct surveys and interviews with potential customers to gather feedback on your value proposition.

Focus Groups: Use focus groups to test different versions of your value proposition and gauge reactions.

2: A/B Testing

Importance: A/B testing allows you to compare different versions of your value proposition to see which performs better.

Methods:

Landing Pages: Create multiple landing pages with different value propositions and track conversion rates.

Email Campaigns: Test different value propositions in email campaigns to measure engagement and response rates.

3: Iterative Refinement

Importance: Continuously refining your value proposition ensures it remains relevant and compelling.

Methods:

Regular Updates: Regularly update your value proposition based on feedback and market changes.

Performance Metrics: Track key performance metrics to evaluate the effectiveness of your value proposition.

Case Study: Slack

Slack's value proposition is a strong example of how to effectively communicate the benefits of a product. Slack identified the problem of inefficient workplace communication and positioned itself as a solution that simplifies and streamlines communication. Their value proposition highlights the benefits of increased productivity, easy collaboration, and integration with other tools. By clearly communicating these benefits and differentiating itself from traditional communication tools, Slack successfully captured a significant share of the market.

Conclusion

Developing a compelling value proposition is a critical step in the entrepreneurial journey. It helps to clearly communicate the unique value your product or service provides, differentiate it from competitors, and convince potential customers of its worth. By understanding the components of a value proposition, crafting a clear and compelling message, and continuously testing and refining it, entrepreneurs can create a strong foundation for their marketing strategies and customer engagement. Through practical steps, methods, and real-world examples, this chapter provides entrepreneurs with the tools and knowledge needed to develop a powerful value proposition that drives business success.

Chapter 15
The Role of Business Models

The Importance of Business Models

A business model is a blueprint for how a company creates, delivers, and captures value. It outlines the strategy and operational structures that guide how a business operates and makes money. A great idea needs a solid business model to succeed, as it provides the foundation for turning an innovative concept into a sustainable and profitable venture. This chapter explores different business models and how to choose the right one for your idea, including subscription, freemium, and platform-based models.

Understanding Business Models

1: Definition of a Business Model

Importance: A business model defines how a company generates revenue and makes a profit.

Components: Key components include value proposition, target market, revenue streams, cost structure, and key activities.

2: Role of a Business Model in Entrepreneurship

Guidance: Provides a roadmap for building and scaling a business.

Clarity: Helps clarify the value offered to customers and how it is delivered.

Sustainability: Ensures the business can sustain itself financially in the long run.

Key Types of Business Models

1: Subscription Model

Overview: Customers pay a recurring fee at regular intervals (monthly, quarterly, annually) to access a product or service.

Benefits:

Predictable Revenue: Ensures a steady stream of income.

Customer Retention: Encourages long-term relationships with customers.

Examples:

Netflix: Offers streaming services for a monthly fee.

SaaS Companies: Software as a Service companies like Salesforce charge subscription fees for access to their software.

2: Freemium Model

Overview: Basic features are offered for free, while advanced features require payment.

Benefits:

User Acquisition: Attracts a large user base with the free offering.

Upselling Opportunities: Converts free users to paying customers over time.

Examples:

Spotify: Offers free access to basic music streaming with ads, and premium features for a fee.

Dropbox: Provides limited storage for free, with options to upgrade for more space and features.

3: Platform-Based Model

Overview: Facilitates exchanges between two or more interdependent groups, usually consumers and producers.

Benefits:

Network Effects: Value increases as more users join the platform.

Scalability: Can scale rapidly as the user base grows.

Examples:

Airbnb: Connects hosts with guests looking for short-term accommodations.

Uber: Connects drivers with passengers needing rides.

Choosing the Right Business Model

1: Evaluating Your Idea

Fit with Value Proposition: Ensure the business model aligns with the value your product or service offers.

Target Market: Consider the preferences and behaviors of your target audience.

Revenue Potential: Assess the potential for generating sustainable revenue.

2: Market Analysis

Competitive Landscape: Analyze competitors to understand what business models they use and identify gaps.

Customer Preferences: Gather insights into what payment and usage models customers prefer.

3: Feasibility and Scalability

Operational Feasibility: Evaluate whether you have the resources and capabilities to implement the chosen business model.

Scalability: Consider how easily the business model can scale as your business grows.

Implementing Your Business Model

1: Building the Infrastructure

Technology and Tools: Invest in the necessary technology and tools to support the business model (e.g., subscription management software).

Processes and Systems: Develop processes and systems to manage operations efficiently.

2: Customer Acquisition and Retention

Marketing Strategies: Develop marketing strategies tailored to the chosen business model.

Customer Support: Ensure robust customer support to maintain high levels of customer satisfaction and retention.

3: Monitoring and Optimization

Key Metrics: Track key performance indicators (KPIs) relevant to your business model (e.g., customer acquisition cost, churn rate, lifetime value).

Continuous Improvement: Regularly review and optimize your business model based on performance data and customer feedback.

Case Studies: Successful Business Models

1: Netflix (Subscription Model)

Success Factors: Predictable revenue stream, extensive content library, and strong customer retention strategies.

Growth Strategy: Continual investment in original content and international expansion.

2: Spotify (Freemium Model)

Success Factors: Large user base from the free tier, high conversion rate to premium, and personalized music recommendations.

Growth Strategy: Expanding features and services, such as podcasts and exclusive content.

3: Airbnb (Platform-Based Model)

Success Factors: Strong network effects, wide variety of listings, and user trust and safety measures.

Growth Strategy: Expanding into new markets and adding experiences and other services.

Conclusion

Choosing the right business model is crucial for the success of any entrepreneurial venture. A well-defined business model provides a clear roadmap for how to create, deliver, and capture value. By understanding different business models, evaluating their fit with your idea, and implementing them effectively, entrepreneurs can build sustainable and profitable businesses. Through practical insights and real-world examples, this chapter equips entrepreneurs with the knowledge and tools needed to choose and implement the right business model for their innovative ideas, ensuring long-term success and growth.

Chapter 16
Storytelling and Pitching

The Importance of Storytelling and Pitching

Effectively communicating your idea is crucial to gaining support from investors, partners, and customers. Storytelling and pitching are essential skills for entrepreneurs, allowing them to convey their vision, passion, and the potential impact of their ideas. This chapter provides tips on how to tell a compelling story and pitch your idea, emphasizing clarity, passion, and impact.

Understanding Storytelling in Business

1: Definition of Storytelling

Importance: Storytelling is the art of using narratives to convey information and connect with an audience emotionally.

Benefits: Engages the audience, makes information memorable, and creates a strong emotional connection.

2: Components of a Compelling Story

Character: The protagonist, often representing the customer or the entrepreneur.

Conflict: The problem or challenge that needs to be solved.

Resolution: The solution offered by the entrepreneur's product or service.

Moral: The key takeaway or lesson that reinforces the value proposition.

Crafting Your Entrepreneurial Story

1: Identify the Core Message

Importance: A clear and focused core message ensures your story is impactful and memorable.

Methods:

Value Proposition: Base your core message on the unique value your idea offers.

Customer Impact: Highlight how your idea will positively affect the lives of customers.

2: Build the Narrative Structure

Importance: A well-structured narrative ensures your story flows logically and keeps the audience engaged.

Methods:

Introduction: Set the stage by introducing the main character and the context.

Conflict: Describe the problem or challenge that needs to be addressed.

Resolution: Present your idea as the solution to the problem.

Conclusion: Conclude with the impact and benefits of your idea, reinforcing the core message.

3: Incorporate Personal Elements

Importance: Personal elements make the story more relatable and authentic.

Methods:

Personal Experience: Share your journey, challenges, and motivations behind the idea.

Customer Stories: Include testimonials or anecdotes from customers who have benefited from your idea.

Effective Pitching Techniques

1: Know Your Audience

Importance: Tailoring your pitch to the audience's interests and needs increases its effectiveness.

Methods:

Research: Understand the background, preferences, and pain points of your audience.

Customization: Adapt your pitch to address the specific concerns and interests of the audience.

1: Craft a Strong Opening

Importance: A compelling opening grabs the audience's attention and sets the tone for the pitch.

Methods:

Hook: Start with a provocative question, surprising fact, or impactful statement.

Relevance: Quickly establish why your idea matters to the audience.

2: Present a Clear Value Proposition

Importance: Clearly articulating the value of your idea helps the audience understand its significance.

Methods:

Problem-Solution-Benefit: Structure your pitch to highlight the problem, your solution, and the benefits.

Visual Aids: Use visuals, such as slides or prototypes, to reinforce key points.

3: Showcase Your Passion and Enthusiasm

Importance: Passion and enthusiasm are contagious and can inspire confidence in your idea.

Methods:

Energy and Emotion: Use energetic delivery and expressive body language.

Personal Connection: Share why you are personally invested in the idea.

4: Provide Evidence and Credibility

Importance: Evidence and credibility enhance the trustworthiness of your pitch.

Methods:

Data and Metrics: Present relevant data, market research, and metrics to support your claims.

Testimonials and Endorsements: Include endorsements from customers, experts, or partners.

5: Handle Questions and Objections Gracefully

Importance: Addressing questions and objections confidently demonstrates preparedness and competence.

Methods:

Anticipate: Prepare for potential questions and objections in advance.

Listen and Respond: Listen carefully to questions and respond thoughtfully and respectfully.

6: End with a Strong Call to Action

Importance: A clear call to action directs the audience on the next steps and reinforces your objective.

Methods:

Specific Request: Clearly state what you are asking for (e.g., investment, partnership, feedback).

Urgency and Relevance: Highlight the urgency and relevance of taking action now.

Practical Steps for Pitch Preparation

1: Develop Your Pitch Deck

Importance: A well-designed pitch deck supports your verbal pitch with visuals and key points.

Components:

Introduction Slide: Overview of your idea and its significance.

Problem Slide: Description of the problem you are addressing.

Solution Slide: Explanation of your solution and its benefits.

Market Opportunity Slide: Market size and growth potential.

Business Model Slide: How you will make money.

Traction Slide: Evidence of progress and success so far.

Team Slide: Introduction to your team and their qualifications.

Financial Projections Slide: Key financial metrics and forecasts.

Call to Action Slide: Clear and compelling call to action.

2: Practice and Refine Your Pitch

Importance: Practice ensures you deliver your pitch confidently and smoothly.

Methods:

Rehearsal: Practice in front of a mirror, with friends, or colleagues.

Feedback: Seek feedback from others and make necessary adjustments.

3: Prepare for Q&A

Importance: Being prepared for questions shows you are thorough and confident.

Methods:

Mock Q&A: Conduct mock Q&A sessions to practice handling questions.

Resource Materials: Have additional materials ready to support your responses if needed.

Case Study: Airbnb

Airbnb's early pitch to investors is a classic example of effective storytelling and pitching. The founders shared their personal story of how they started Airbnb to solve their own problem of affording rent. They presented a clear problem (inadequate and expensive accommodations for travelers), their innovative solution (an online platform for short-term rentals), and compelling evidence (early traction and user testimonials). Their passion, clarity, and the compelling narrative helped them secure crucial early funding and support.

Conclusion

Storytelling and pitching are vital skills for entrepreneurs, enabling them to effectively communicate their ideas and gain support from investors, partners, and customers. By crafting a compelling story, understanding your audience, and employing effective pitching techniques, you can present your idea with clarity, passion, and impact. Through practical tips and real-world examples, this chapter provides entrepreneurs with the tools and knowledge needed to master storytelling and pitching, ensuring their ideas are heard, understood, and supported.

Chapter 17
Building an Idea Generation Framework

The Importance of a Structured Approach

Consistently generating high-quality ideas requires more than just creativity; it demands a structured approach that ensures a steady flow of innovative concepts. A well-defined framework helps entrepreneurs systematically generate, evaluate, and refine ideas, making the process more efficient and effective. This chapter introduces frameworks and processes for systematically generating and evaluating ideas, including the Lean Startup methodology and Design Thinking.

Understanding Idea Generation Frameworks

1: Definition of an Idea Generation Framework

Importance: A structured approach to generating, evaluating, and refining ideas.

Benefits: Increases consistency, efficiency, and the likelihood of generating viable ideas.

2: Components of an Effective Framework

Ideation: Techniques for generating a wide range of ideas.

Evaluation: Criteria and methods for assessing the feasibility and potential of ideas.

Refinement: Processes for iterating and improving ideas based on feedback and testing.

The Lean Startup Methodology

1: Overview of Lean Startup

Definition: A methodology that emphasizes rapid experimentation, validated learning, and iterative development.

Origin: Developed by Eric Ries, based on principles from lean manufacturing.

2: Key Principles of Lean Startup

Build-Measure-Learn Cycle: A loop of creating a minimum viable product (MVP), measuring its performance, and learning from the results.

Validated Learning: Using data and feedback to validate assumptions and refine ideas.

Pivot or Persevere: Deciding whether to pivot (change direction) or persevere (continue on the current path) based on feedback.

3: Implementing Lean Startup for Idea Generation

Step 1: Ideation

Brainstorming: Generate a wide range of ideas without immediate judgment.

Problem Identification: Focus on identifying and solving specific problems.

Step 2: Build (MVP)

Prototyping: Create a simple version of the product or service to test key assumptions.

Step 3: Measure

Customer Feedback: Collect data from potential users through surveys, interviews, and usage analytics.

Step 4: Learn

Analysis: Analyze feedback to validate or invalidate assumptions.

Iteration: Refine the idea based on what was learned and repeat the cycle.

Design Thinking

1: Overview of Design Thinking

Definition: A human-centered approach to innovation that focuses on understanding users, defining problems, and creating effective solutions.

Origin: Popularized by IDEO and Stanford's d.school.

1: Key Stages of Design Thinking

Empathize: Understand the needs, behaviors, and emotions of the users.

Define: Clearly articulate the problem to be solved.

Ideate: Generate a broad range of ideas and solutions.

Prototype: Build tangible representations of ideas to explore their viability.

Test: Gather feedback from users to refine and improve prototypes.

2: Implementing Design Thinking for Idea Generation

Stage 1: Empathize

User Research: Conduct interviews, observations, and surveys to gather insights.

Stage 2: Define

Problem Statement: Create a clear and concise problem statement based on user insights.

Stage 3: Ideate

Brainstorming Sessions: Conduct collaborative brainstorming sessions to generate diverse ideas.

Creative Techniques: Use methods like mind mapping, SCAMPER, and reverse brainstorming.

Stage 4: Prototype

Rapid Prototyping: Develop quick and inexpensive prototypes to explore different aspects of the ideas.

Stage 5: Test

User Testing: Present prototypes to users and gather feedback.

Iteration: Refine ideas and prototypes based on user feedback and repeat the cycle.

Combining Lean Startup and Design Thinking

Complementary Approaches

Lean Startup: Focuses on rapid iteration and validated learning.

Design Thinking: Emphasizes empathy and human-centered design.

Synergy: Combining both approaches can enhance the effectiveness of idea generation by ensuring that solutions are both innovative and user-centered.

3: Integrating Both Frameworks

Empathize and Define (Design Thinking)

Understand Users: Use Design Thinking to deeply understand users and define problems.

Ideate and Prototype (Design Thinking and Lean Startup)

Generate Ideas: Use Design Thinking techniques to generate ideas.

Build MVPs: Apply Lean Startup principles to develop minimum viable products.

Test and Learn (Lean Startup)

Validate Assumptions: Use Lean Startup methods to test and validate assumptions with real users.

Iterate: Iterate based on feedback, combining insights from both frameworks.

Creating Your Custom Idea Generation Framework

1: Assess Your Needs and Goals

Importance: Tailoring the framework to your specific context ensures relevance and effectiveness.

Methods:

Identify Objectives: Define what you aim to achieve with your idea generation efforts.

Evaluate Resources: Assess the resources available, such as time, budget, and team expertise.

2: Select Appropriate Techniques

Importance: Choosing the right techniques ensures that your framework is effective and manageable.

Methods:

Combination of Techniques: Select a combination of techniques from Lean Startup, Design Thinking, and other methodologies.

Adaptation: Adapt techniques to fit your specific context and needs.

3: Implement and Iterate

Importance: Implementation and continuous improvement ensure the framework remains effective.

Methods:

Pilot Testing: Start with a pilot test to refine the framework.

Feedback and Adjustment: Gather feedback from the team and stakeholders, and adjust the framework as needed.

Case Study: Airbnb's Use of Frameworks

Airbnb's success can be attributed to its effective use of both Lean Startup and Design Thinking principles. The founders started with a clear understanding of the problem (expensive and inadequate lodging for travelers) and deeply empathized with potential users. They used rapid prototyping to create an MVP, tested it with real users, and iterated based on feedback. This combination of human-centered design and validated learning helped Airbnb refine its value proposition and scale successfully.

Conclusion

Building an idea generation framework is crucial for consistently generating and evaluating innovative ideas. By understanding and implementing structured approaches like Lean Startup and Design Thinking, entrepreneurs can enhance their creativity, efficiency, and the likelihood of success. Through practical insights and real-world examples, this chapter provides entrepreneurs with the tools and knowledge needed to create a customized idea generation framework that drives sustained innovation and business growth.

Chapter 18
Overcoming Creative Blocks

Understanding Creative Blocks

Creative blocks are a common challenge faced by entrepreneurs. These blocks can hinder the flow of innovative ideas and stall progress. Recognizing the signs of a creative block and understanding its root causes are essential first steps in overcoming these obstacles.

1: Definition of Creative Blocks

Importance: Creative blocks are mental barriers that impede the flow of ideas and creative thinking.

Signs: Symptoms include lack of inspiration, difficulty focusing, and a sense of being stuck or overwhelmed.

2: Causes of Creative Blocks

Mental Fatigue: Prolonged periods of intense focus and work can lead to burnout.

Fear of Failure: Anxiety about making mistakes can stifle creativity.

Perfectionism: The desire to create something perfect can prevent progress.

Environmental Factors: Distractions and an uninspiring environment can hinder creativity.

Strategies for Overcoming Creative Blocks

1: Taking Breaks

Importance: Breaks help refresh the mind, reduce stress, and restore mental energy.

Methods:

Short Breaks: Take brief, regular breaks throughout the day to prevent mental fatigue.

Extended Breaks: Consider taking a longer break or a vacation to recharge completely.

2: Changing Environments

Importance: A new environment can stimulate fresh perspectives and ideas.

Methods:

Workspaces: Move to a different room, work in a park, or visit a café.

Nature: Spend time outdoors to benefit from the calming and inspiring effects of nature.

3: Seeking Inspiration

Importance: Exposure to new ideas and experiences can spark creativity.

Methods:

Reading: Explore books, articles, and blogs on various topics.

Art and Culture: Visit museums, attend cultural events, or watch inspiring films.

Conversations: Engage in discussions with people from different backgrounds and industries.

4: Mindfulness and Meditation

Importance: Mindfulness and meditation practices can reduce stress and enhance mental clarity.

Methods:

Breathing Exercises: Practice deep breathing exercises to relax the mind.

Guided Meditation: Use apps or videos to engage in guided meditation sessions.

5: Physical Activity

Importance: Exercise boosts endorphins and enhances mental clarity.

Methods:

Regular Exercise: Incorporate physical activities such as jogging, yoga, or swimming into your routine.

Movement Breaks: Take short breaks to stretch or walk around.

6: Creative Exercises

Importance: Specific exercises can stimulate creative thinking and break mental barriers.

Methods:

Free Writing: Write continuously for a set period without worrying about grammar or structure.

Mind Mapping: Create visual diagrams to explore and connect ideas.

Brainstorming Games: Use games and prompts to generate ideas in a fun and relaxed manner.

7: Embracing Failure and Imperfection

Importance: Accepting failure and imperfection can alleviate pressure and encourage experimentation.

Methods:

Small Experiments: Conduct small, low-stakes experiments to test ideas.

Learning Mindset: Focus on learning and growth rather than perfection.

8: Setting Realistic Goals

Importance: Realistic and achievable goals can reduce overwhelm and increase motivation.

Methods:

SMART Goals: Set Specific, Measurable, Achievable, Relevant, and Time-bound goals.

Incremental Steps: Break larger tasks into smaller, manageable steps.

Practical Techniques for Everyday Creativity

1: Daily Creative Routine

Importance: Consistency can build momentum and make creativity a habit.

Methods:

Dedicated Time: Set aside specific times each day for creative work.

Rituals: Develop rituals that signal the start of your creative time (e.g., a cup of tea, a specific playlist).

2: Journaling

Importance: Journaling can help process thoughts and generate new ideas.

Methods:

Daily Entries: Write daily entries about your thoughts, ideas, and experiences.

Prompt-Based Journaling: Use prompts to explore different aspects of your work and life.

3: Collaborative Creativity

Importance: Collaborating with others can provide new perspectives and ideas.

Methods:

Brainstorming Sessions: Regularly hold brainstorming sessions with colleagues or peers.

Feedback Loops: Establish feedback loops to continuously refine and improve ideas.

Case Study: Overcoming Creative Blocks at Pixar

Pixar, renowned for its creativity and innovation, has developed several strategies to overcome creative blocks. One notable practice is their "Braintrust" sessions, where directors present their work to a group of peers who provide candid feedback. This collaborative environment encourages fresh ideas and continuous improvement. Additionally, Pixar emphasizes the importance of a creative work environment, offering spaces designed to inspire creativity and collaboration.

Conclusion

Creative blocks are a natural part of the entrepreneurial journey, but they can be overcome with the right strategies. By taking breaks, changing environments, seeking inspiration, practicing mindfulness, engaging in physical activity, and embracing failure, entrepreneurs can overcome these obstacles and maintain a steady flow of innovative ideas. Through practical techniques and real-world examples, this chapter provides entrepreneurs with the tools and knowledge needed to navigate and overcome creative blocks, ensuring sustained creativity and progress.

Chapter 19
Case Studies of Successful Entrepreneurs

The Power of Learning from Success

Understanding how successful entrepreneurs have generated and developed their ideas can provide invaluable insights and inspiration. This chapter presents case studies of renowned entrepreneurs, highlighting the idea generation techniques they employed to build their businesses. These stories illustrate diverse strategies and methodologies, showcasing the importance of adaptability, creativity, and perseverance in entrepreneurship.

Case Study 1: Steve Jobs and Apple

1: Background

Entrepreneur: Steve Jobs

Company: Apple Inc.

Industry: Technology

2: Idea Generation Techniques

User-Centered Design: Jobs emphasized designing products with the end user in mind. His focus on intuitive, user-friendly interfaces set Apple apart.

Observation and Empathy: Jobs spent time understanding how people interacted with technology, identifying pain points and areas for improvement.

Collaboration: He collaborated closely with designers and engineers, fostering an environment of innovation and creativity.

3: Key Innovations

iPod: Revolutionized the music industry with a portable, user-friendly digital music player.

iPhone: Transformed the smartphone market with its touch interface, sleek design, and powerful functionality.

iPad: Created a new category of devices, blending the functionality of a laptop and the portability of a smartphone.

Case Study 2: Sara Blakely and Spanx

1: Background

Entrepreneur: Sara Blakely

Company: Spanx

Industry: Fashion/Undergarments

2: Idea Generation Techniques

Personal Experience: Blakely identified a personal pain point—uncomfortable and unflattering undergarments—and sought to solve it.

Prototyping: She created the first prototype of Spanx by cutting the feet off her pantyhose.

Market Research: Blakely conducted extensive market research, speaking directly with potential customers to understand their needs.

1: Key Innovations

Footless Pantyhose: Introduced a more comfortable, versatile undergarment that smoothed the appearance of the wearer.

Product Line Expansion: Expanded the product line to include a variety of shapewear, maintaining a focus on comfort and functionality.

Case Study 3: Elon Musk and SpaceX

1: Background

Entrepreneur: Elon Musk

Company: SpaceX

Industry: Aerospace

2: Idea Generation Techniques

Visionary Thinking: Musk envisioned a future where space travel was accessible and sustainable, driving his innovative pursuits.

Cross-Industry Innovation: Applied principles from software engineering and automotive manufacturing to aerospace.

Iterative Development: Adopted a trial-and-error approach, rapidly prototyping and testing to refine ideas.

3: Key Innovations

Reusable Rockets: Developed rockets that could be reused multiple times, drastically reducing the cost of space travel.

Falcon Heavy: Created one of the most powerful operational rockets, capable of carrying large payloads into space.

Starship: Working towards a fully reusable spacecraft designed for missions to Mars and beyond.

Case Study 4: Oprah Winfrey and Harpo Productions

1: Background

Entrepreneur: Oprah Winfrey

Company: Harpo Productions

Industry: Media and Entertainment

2: Idea Generation Techniques

Empathy and Connection: Winfrey's ability to connect with her audience on an emotional level drove her content creation.

Audience Feedback: She continuously gathered and responded to audience feedback, tailoring her content to meet their interests and needs.

Personal Branding: Leveraged her personal brand to build trust and loyalty, expanding into various media formats.

3: Key Innovations

The Oprah Winfrey Show: Became one of the highest-rated talk shows, known for its impactful interviews and inspirational content.

OWN Network: Launched her own cable network, providing a platform for diverse and meaningful programming.

Oprah's Book Club: Influenced the literary world by recommending and discussing books, significantly boosting their sales.

Case Study 5: Jeff Bezos and Amazon

1: Background

Entrepreneur: Jeff Bezos

Company: Amazon

Industry: E-commerce and Technology

2: Idea Generation Techniques

Customer-Centric Approach: Bezos prioritized customer satisfaction, constantly seeking ways to enhance the shopping experience.

Long-Term Vision: Focused on long-term goals and investments, even at the expense of short-term profits.

Data-Driven Decisions: Utilized data and analytics to inform decisions and drive innovation.

3: Key Innovations

Online Marketplace: Revolutionized retail with an extensive online marketplace offering a vast selection of products.

Amazon Prime: Introduced a subscription service that provided fast shipping and exclusive content, increasing customer loyalty.

AWS (Amazon Web Services): Diversified into cloud computing, becoming a leading provider of cloud infrastructure services.

Case Study 6: Brian Chesky and Airbnb

1: Background

Entrepreneur: Brian Chesky

Company: Airbnb

Industry: Hospitality and Travel

2: Idea Generation Techniques

Solving Personal Problems: Chesky and his co-founders created Airbnb to solve their own problem of affording rent by renting out air mattresses in their apartment.

Community Feedback: Engaged with early users to gather feedback and refine the platform.

Iterative Testing: Continuously tested and iterated on the platform, improving functionality and user experience.

3: Key Innovations

Peer-to-Peer Lodging: Pioneered a platform for people to rent out their homes or spare rooms to travelers.

Experiences: Expanded offerings to include local experiences and activities hosted by residents.

Trust and Safety Features: Developed robust trust and safety measures to build confidence among hosts and guests.

Conclusion

Studying the successes of other entrepreneurs can provide valuable lessons and inspiration. The case studies of Steve Jobs, Sara Blakely, Elon Musk, Oprah Winfrey, Jeff Bezos, and Brian Chesky highlight diverse idea generation techniques, from user-centered design and personal experience to visionary thinking and customer-centric approaches. By learning from these successful entrepreneurs, aspiring business owners can gain insights into effective strategies for generating and developing their own innovative ideas. Through practical examples and real-world applications, this chapter offers entrepreneurs the tools and knowledge needed to emulate and adapt these successful techniques in their own ventures.

Chapter 20
Continuous Improvement and Adaptation

The Ever-Evolving Nature of Entrepreneurship

In entrepreneurship, the journey of idea generation and business development is never truly complete. Markets evolve, technologies advance, and consumer preferences shift, necessitating a continuous cycle of improvement and adaptation. This chapter underscores the importance of maintaining an agile mindset, fostering a culture of continuous learning, and staying responsive to change to ensure long-term success.

The Philosophy of Continuous Improvement

1: Definition and Importance

Continuous Improvement: A systematic, ongoing effort to enhance products, services, or processes.

Significance: Helps businesses stay competitive, meet evolving customer needs, and capitalize on new opportunities.

2: Key Principles

Incremental Changes: Small, regular improvements can accumulate to create significant advancements over time.

Feedback Loops: Consistent collection and analysis of feedback to guide improvement efforts.

Proactive Adaptation: Anticipating and responding to changes in the market or technology landscape.

Frameworks for Continuous Improvement

1: Kaizen

Origin: A Japanese term meaning "change for better," widely used in lean manufacturing.

Principles: Focus on small, incremental improvements involving all employees.

Application: Implement daily or weekly reviews of processes and encourage employee suggestions for improvements.

2: Six Sigma

Origin: A set of techniques and tools for process improvement, developed by Motorola.

Principles: Data-driven approach aiming for near-perfection in processes.

Application: Use DMAIC (Define, Measure, Analyze, Improve, Control) methodology to identify and eliminate defects.

3: Agile Methodology

Origin: Developed for software development, emphasizing iterative progress and collaboration.

Principles: Flexibility, customer feedback, and incremental delivery.

Application: Regularly review and adjust product features and development processes based on stakeholder feedback.

Techniques for Adaptation

1: Market Research and Trend Analysis

Importance: Understanding market dynamics and emerging trends helps businesses stay relevant.

Methods: Regularly conduct surveys, focus groups, and competitive analysis to gather insights.

2: Customer Feedback

Importance: Direct feedback from customers provides actionable insights for improvement.

Methods: Use customer surveys, reviews, and social media monitoring to gather and analyze feedback.

3: Benchmarking

Importance: Comparing your business against industry leaders can highlight areas for improvement.

Methods: Identify key performance indicators (KPIs) and measure your performance against top competitors.

The Role of Technology in Continuous Improvement

1: Data Analytics

Importance: Data-driven decision-making enhances precision in improvement efforts.

Methods: Use analytics tools to gather, process, and analyze data from various sources.

2: Artificial Intelligence and Machine Learning

Importance: AI and ML can uncover patterns and predict trends, informing strategic decisions.

Methods: Implement AI-driven tools for customer insights, demand forecasting, and process optimization.

3: Automation

Importance: Automating repetitive tasks increases efficiency and allows focus on strategic activities.

Methods: Utilize automation tools for marketing, customer service, and supply chain management.

Building a Culture of Continuous Improvement

1: Leadership and Vision

Importance: Leadership plays a crucial role in fostering a culture of continuous improvement.

Methods: Leaders should communicate a clear vision, set expectations, and lead by example.

2: Employee Involvement

Importance: Engaging employees at all levels promotes a sense of ownership and innovation.

Methods: Create platforms for employees to share ideas, provide feedback, and participate in improvement initiatives.

3: Training and Development

Importance: Ongoing education ensures employees have the skills and knowledge to contribute effectively.

Methods: Offer regular training programs, workshops, and access to learning resources.

Case Study: Toyota's Commitment to Kaizen

1: Background

Company: Toyota

Industry: Automotive

2: Implementation of Kaizen

Employee Empowerment: Toyota empowers all employees to identify areas for improvement and implement changes.

Continuous Feedback: Regularly collects and acts on feedback from employees and customers.

Incremental Improvements: Focuses on making small, incremental changes across all processes, resulting in significant long-term advancements.

3: Results

Operational Efficiency: Enhanced production efficiency and reduced waste.

Product Quality: Improved product quality and customer satisfaction.

Innovation: Maintained a competitive edge through continuous innovation.

Embracing Change and Future-Proofing Your Business

1: Anticipating Change

Importance: Being proactive about future trends and potential disruptions helps businesses stay ahead.

Methods: Regularly conduct scenario planning and strategic forecasting.

2: Agility and Flexibility

Importance: Agile businesses can quickly adapt to changes and seize new opportunities.

Methods: Implement flexible processes and maintain a readiness to pivot when necessary.

3: Innovation and Experimentation

Importance: Constant innovation is key to staying relevant and competitive.

Methods: Encourage experimentation, pilot new ideas, and embrace a fail-fast mentality.

Conclusion

The journey of idea generation and business development is ongoing. Continuous improvement and adaptation are essential for long-term success in the ever-evolving world of entrepreneurship. By adopting a mindset of continuous learning, leveraging frameworks like Kaizen, Six Sigma, and Agile, and embracing technological advancements, entrepreneurs can stay responsive to change and maintain a competitive edge. Through practical insights and real-world examples, this chapter equips entrepreneurs with the tools and strategies needed to foster a culture of continuous improvement, ensuring sustained innovation and business growth.

www.ingramcontent.com/pod-product-compliance
Lightning Source LLC
Chambersburg PA
CBHW071923210526
45479CB00002B/530